All writings of truth are not the Truth
They are about the Truth

We just give them meaning which makes them

Symbols of Power [1]

---

[1] All disciplines of learning, i.e. psychology, sociology, philosophy, theology, politics, economics, ecology and education, etc., are built on and sustained by the meanings you have given them. Society is *a collective hunch;* conditioned thinking built upon layers of meanings made sacred over time.

Symbols of Power

A Guide to Facilitate Healing
by
Mathias Karayan

A companion manual to:
The Way Home; Stories from the Master

Cover design by Rachael Balsaitis
Layout by Barbara Campbell

Library of Congress Control Number
2011900517

ISBN: 978-0-9820675-3-6

Acknowledgement

To Jackie Jeffery; thank you for your dedication to keeping this material internally consistent.

To Cory Yenor; who, when I would doubt myself, reminded me of the relevance of this material.

To Michael Weinaur, Annalicia Niemela, Lynda Kay Johnson; my friends in Spirit.

To Kate Evans and Maria Monterey; for your insights.

Dedication

To Rita,
My intuitive sweetheart
You remind me that the whirlwind is just a dance

Those who think they live in space and time
relate to and communicate through
the symbols of space and time

It is through the intention of love that I write
about the experience of the eternal

Using the symbols of space and time

Matt Karayan
December 2011

TABLE OF CONTENTS

Section I

Symbols of Power
and
Life's Continuity

Section II

Symbols of Power
and
Your Creative Self

Introduction

Religion in all its forms is the expression of one's search to reunite with Spirit. The body, properly perceived, can be used as a means for healing; a tool to once again hear Spirit's call. Likewise, all psychic, supernatural, out of body and miraculous experiences are expressions of a consciousness beyond the body's senses. Though they are temporary in nature, they can be used as aids to break through your beliefs about a world untrue . . . to remember You as Spirit.

Beyond your beliefs about a world untrue is your memory of Spirit, an experience you already know. You use your beliefs to block that memory. You are but a thought away from remembering. Therefore, all beliefs about ever-changing forms are your symbols of power that can limit your mind to a temporary experience[2] or free you to remember your Eternal Self.

This book is for those who consciously practice to facilitate healing; for themselves and for their client. It contains clarifications of some symbols of "the new age" that have been interpreted to enslave your mind to limits of experience. Because all symbols are temporary in nature, the teaching principles in this book can be generalized to *all disciplines* of thought.

The curriculum presented in this book is in direct opposition to the world's curriculum. The world teaches you to be a better judge for decision. This curriculum teaches that to relinquish judgment is your journey to freedom, for it is your beliefs about a world untrue that has enslaved you.[3]

---

[2]The definition of all sickness.

[3]For those who say "You have to have judgments to survive or to operate in the world," are those who believe their judgments protect them. This book will suggest that *your judgments are the cause of your fears!*

To judge is to invite conflict

*To relinquish judgment is to allow
peace of mind to be itself*

The world's judgments are blocks, substitutes, symbols, mediating forms of beliefs that limit you to the experience of a duality of thought . . . thoughts that bring you conflict and fear. This book is an approach to help you relinquish judgment; to remember your creative Self with Source . . . should you so choose.

Checkmate

"And now I look out from my mountain
And see the soldiers in the field
It won't be long now till they'll have me
This time advance guards are for real

Come on, come on
Take me there, take me there – I don't care where we go
Take me, I just want to know what I used to know"

Advance Guards
James Seals

Section I

Symbols of Power
and
Life's Continuity

The Beginning is the place you've already been

*Moving forward is the illusion of
wanting to remember the beginning*

Today is but a ripple of that place out of time

What Healing Is
and How It Is Accomplished

No symbol has power over you
except the power you give it

And this you can change

Introduction

No one heals anyone but themselves. Even this idea contains fallacy because all healing is of Source, who does not know sickness. Healer, what a strange situation you find yourself in. Your work is to facilitate healing for those who perceive themselves as sick . . . so you can wake up!

Healer, because the body dies
"Heal thyself" means what?

Three Points for Reflection

Before you can facilitate healing with someone who perceives themselves as sick, there are three points to reflect on that are important for consideration.

The understanding that;
  1) No symbol has power[4] over you except the power you give it.

And the questions of clarification that ask:
  2) What are the symbols of power I employ in my life?
  3) Do these symbols enslave me or do they free me?[5]

---

[4]All beliefs, judgments, substitutions, mediating forms are symbols of power you hold dear.

[5]*Everything* you use in your world symbolizes an idol; a defense against your awareness of personal peace, or a messenger of healing because it leads you beyond all symbols, towards peace of mind.

The honest consideration of these three points and the *consistent application* of the next five distinctions make all the difference between being an unhealed healer or a healed healer.

Five Distinctions

When your client comes to you for help, it will be obvious that;

1) *The problem:* They have empowered symbols[6] that enslave their mind to limits of experience.[7] In other words, they experience only what they choose to believe. *This is the definition of sickness.*

2) *The cause of sickness:* Your client is the cause of their own sickness.[8] They have given their power to conflicting beliefs that are the cause of all their conflicts.

3) *The clarification:* Because the body dies, "Heal Thyself" cannot mean heal the body.[9] In the final analysis, sickness and health have nothing to do with a body. *Healing is always about and for the mind.*

4) *The goal:* The goal must be peace of mind because peace of mind is the only goal that transcends the conflicting symbols your client has empowered to enslave their mind to the limits of a body that will die.[10]

---

[6] Beliefs, judgments, substitutions that your client plays out in various forms.

[7] Selective perception.

[8] We all look for solutions outside of ourselves (placebos, substitutions) until we no longer fear to look within. *The Way Home; p49-52*

[9] "I do not deny that in your experience of a world, healings of the body seem to occur. But if your primary goal is to heal the body, in the end it will fail you and die. Do not fear. For you are more than the body you appear to inhabit." *The Way Home; p162-165*

[10] That the body can be ill and die is not sickness. That is what the body does. Sickness is your ability to deceive yourself into believing that you are the limits of a body.

5) *The means to healing:* Because your client has empowered symbols that limit experience, they also have the power to change their mind about them. This makes your client their own means for healing.

The Practitioner's Role

*The exceptional teacher is one whose students say
"I have no need of this anymore"*

The proper role of all practitioners to facilitate healing is to reframe all symbols of power your client presents so they can eventually understand that healing comes from within. Healer, be aware. They come to you for a reason. Therefore, you become a mediating form and thus a symbol of power. Allow for no dependency to occur or you become just another idol for them.

Knowing is mind's natural disposition. All symbols that limit your mind, limit it from the experience of knowing. To not know is to experience doubt and thus a world of belief.[11] Because your beliefs block your experience of Being, they reinforce the deception that you are something you are not. What else could you experience from self deception but anger, guilt and fear? Your client's defense from guilt and fear is a denial that projects it as something coming from the outside. Now it is removed from the solution. The solution is not to be found in the world. It is in the mind that made guilt and fear seem real. If you are not aware of your projection, you will interpret the guilt and fear that you put outside of you as attack. Given this dilemma, *it becomes the healer's responsibility to interpret for their client the perception of attack, that seems to be coming from outside themself as an*

---

[11] Or dream state.

opportunity to heal. The therapeutic form[12] used is irrelevant when it is used as an opportunity to undo any idea of attack as real.

The unhealed healer is one who cannot see beyond their own misinterpretations as attack. They, like the client they are trying to help, are unknowingly enslaved by their own symbols of power. Teacher, facilitating opportunities for healing has only one requirement: humility.

> *Don't think you know the way*
> *For if you did you would not be here!*

Enlightenment is waking up! Not evolving into. Be not deceived by the world's definition of enlightenment. To wake up is to be free of all judgment and guilt.

The Client's Role

When your client understands that it is in their best interest to see the problem as an opportunity to heal, they will change the way they perceive it. *Through the repetition of application,* your client learns that it is in their best interest to perceive all conflict as an opportunity to heal.[13] It is only a matter of generalizing the lesson learned to all areas of their life. If your client chooses to hold onto interpretations that engender anger, guilt and fear, they are not ready to hear the call for healing. They will have to wait for the mediating form[14] that does not threaten their chosen world view. Their readiness will allow for the next lesson in a form they can recognize and accept.

---

[12] The mediating symbol of power / placebo / i.e. snake oil medicine.
[13] *The Way Home; p105-107*
[14] Symbol / belief.

A miracle is the experience of peace provided by a mediating form. A miracle is a change of mind, a withdrawal of value from a particular belief that has blocked you from your experience of peace of mind. *This is the only value any symbol has.*[15]

The fear of healing which includes anger, guilt, pain, pleasure and depression are symptoms of beliefs your client holds dear. Your client holds these beliefs dear because they believe they will save them from the anger, guilt and fear that they actually cause.[16] Their denial is the refusal to see that what they think will bring peace of mind is actually causing fear. Your client's greatest need is the courage to understand that they do not really know what they think they know.[17] Facilitator of healing; pace yourself with the client's process of unfolding.

Your Client as a Teacher

Healer, how often have you deceived yourself into making nothing mean something it isn't?[18] Your client can remind you of this when you see through their presenting problem for what it really is . . . a figment of their imagination . . . a mis-thought merely needing correction. Therefore, don't forget your clients are also your teachers. They come to you for healing. Let their experiences facilitate healing for you as well! It will be for the healed healer to help the client identify

---

[15] *The Way Home; p62-64*

[16] This is what makes symbols sacred idols. Any symbol in need of protection is an idol because Truth needs no defense.

[17] This is the only useful thing fear can teach you. In this way you can transform any experience of fear into a call for love. *The Way Home; p53*

[18] The road is treacherous for those who do not know that they are lost to their own chosen road signs.

these limits / symbols / blocks so they can be reinterpreted as a means for healing.[19]

Summary

Your solution is always in the same place where the problem was made, in the mind that thought it. A mind that is divided in its goal is a sick mind. The goal is *unified* when it is *only* peace of mind. The miracle is a way for you and your client to remove the blocks that keep you from remembering the experience of this peace. Healer;

For a while, as a teacher
You need to use the symbols of the world
But in your practice do not be deceived by them
For they do not stand for anything
And in this thought alone will you be released from them

---

[19]The art of healing is not something you can control. The outcome is never because of you. Remember, all healing is of Source who does not know sickness.

Teachers of Healing

The healed healer stands as a light beyond the dream

Introduction

Teachers of healing, you are not asked to go beyond all symbols the world offers, for you still have work to do. You need to use the symbols the world understands for meaning so you can communicate with those you meet along your way. Be not deceived by them anymore for they do not stand for anything. For the experience of One Mind cannot be found in them.

Your Need

Therapist, if you can help your clients to see that *they experience what they first think*, they can heal. If you allow for no exceptions, your client will come to understand that *they are the cause* of the world they experience. In other words, sickness did not choose them, they chose sickness. A sick mind is not open-minded on this point. However, if they chose sickness, they can choose again! You will heal along with them when you remember;

> *No symbol has power over you*
> *except the power you give it*
> *And this you can change*

Therefore, when you recognize that you interpret the world through what you first believe, you come to realize that your need is not to forgive the other for what they did to you. *Your need is to forgive yourself for how you decided to interpret what you thought another did to you.*[20] Not only will you

---

[20] This is the principle of radical forgiveness.

recognize the power your mind has to deceive itself, but you will also recognize the power your mind has to free itself from the reoccurring experience of lessons presented in different forms. These forms are the same lesson waiting for you to forgive your perception of what never was.

"I am deceived by nothing in a form I desire" [21]

Teachers, you have a commission to fulfill. Be diligent to understand what meanings you give to the symbols of form you choose. Let no form be a deception to delay release for your mind or you will teach delay to your client.

You can't teach what you do not know
But you always teach what you think you know

Summary

Healers, you may have spiritual revelations, psychic experiences, and glimpses of enlightenment. You are waking from a long deep slumber, slowly shaking off the depths of despair, a drunken withdrawal, a feverish nightmare, the last frost of winter. Slowly you are being gently nudged . . . into a peaceful calm, a restful sleep . . . eventually to awaken into the arms of Love with a joyous realization that you never left.

Be patient with yourself.[22] Be patient with your client. They come to teach you an ancient lesson forgotten through eons of time. Your journey through is not by the reinforcing of what you thought another did to you. *Your need is to forgive yourself for how you decided to interpret what you thought another did to you.* Teach this to your client so you can learn it. You do

---

[21] A Course In Miracles.
[22] *The Way Home; p100*

not journey alone to your awakening because you journey back to You, the experience of One Mind. In the mean time;

Because denial is massive
Repetition becomes your best teacher [23]

---

[23] *The Way Home; p171*

Beyond the Senses

*Source is known to the mind, not the senses
And as long as the mind is led by the senses
You cannot know Source*

Introduction

Brain is a function of body.[24] Mind is a function used by Spirit for expression. Your mind perceives. Mind interprets its perception of body sensations as either something to desire or something to avoid, thus pleasure and pain. Within the body's realm of pleasure and pain is the experience of birth and death. This makes a body as an end in itself. When mind takes on a body as a self, the expression and memory of Spirit is blocked by the interference of the body's senses. Just below the conscious level, you are choosing continuously.

To know is to experience Self as Source's creation. To believe is to experience something else . . . an individual body in a world of change. This is where your journey began. *Placing the body you think you are into proper perspective is paramount in understanding how to journey home.* You may resist [25] what follows. Be open to another possibility.

---

[24] Mind and brain are two different things. The body's brain (physiology) belongs to the body. To study the brain as if it is mind is senseless confusion.

[25] Resistance is the ego's tactic of diversion. It is a maneuver signifying a desire not to know because its existence is at stake. Its last fierce defense for existence wants you to believe you are a body . . . right up to the body's death.

A Moment of Thoughtlessness

You see only what you wish for
Out of desire you were born to die [26]

In an instant of thoughtlessness[27] mind entertained a thought separate from Source. Through this thought consciousness was made. Consciousness, viewing itself as separate[28] from its Source, divided into a consciousness of many. The idea of a separation that could never be, was thoughtless mind's detour into confusion, self-deception and fear.[29] To protect itself from the fear of a separation that could never be, your mind defined its separateness as an identity, an ego made out of a collection of related thoughts.

Ego, in an attempt to survive, searches for a place to reside, to explain its experience of confusion and justify its fear as real. Through the power and projection of a confused mind, ego slipped in, reached through, and made an earthen vessel (ephemeral body) to hide behind. Surprised in the delight of this association with a body sensation, your mind found gratification of pleasure. As your mind became drunk with pleasure, pain was never far behind. In an attempt to avoid pain, pleasure through the body became the goal. Because the only thing pleasure invites is pain, *your life becomes a preoccupation to achieve pleasurable experiences*

---

[26] Death is but a symbol for separation, nothing more.

[27] This instant of thoughtlessness seems a long time ago only because it has been buried under eons of beliefs with the hope of being forgotten.

[28] The beginning of dualistic thinking; I – You / subject - object.

[29] In terms of Christian theology this is the "original sin," the loss of innocence, the fall from the Garden of Eden. In psychological terminology, this is the source of all "separation anxiety." In existential philosophy this is the human dilemma of "being."

and avoid pain. Anger, grieving, guilt, fear and despair are always waiting just below this conscious level.

Not only did mind use a body as a self idea to defend an individual consciousness that would be subject to physical pain, it also made a world of space, time, movement and noise to hide behind the thought of a separation that could never be. Thus, a world was made by an impossible thought,[30] divided as a collection of separate minds, unknown to Source. This impossible thought is the primary experience a mind lost in self-deception[31] vigorously defends . . . as the only experience that is real.

Because truth needs no justification
A body is needed to defend your self-deception
Your biggest symbol of power is the body
you seem to inhabit

Communication Lost

You sacrificed the experience of knowing communication as One Mind when you chose a thought separate from Source. Your preoccupation with the body you think you are is the primary block you employ to prevent remembering your relationship of knowing. Because knowing was denied through the choices consciousness provides, doubt, belief and faith became the norm[32] as you entered into the night-mare of dualistic thinking. Everything on earth is subject to differing points of view, interpretation and change. It is self-

---

[30] This explains why there is only one ego.

[31] You think you are a separate individual because you seem to be a body. However, the fact of the matter *hidden from your view* is that you actually think you are a body because you first thought your self to be a separate individual.

[32] All substitutes for knowing.

deception to attribute certainty to anything . . . religion, politics, morality, ethics, etc. All of this is played out as the making of human history.

"You believe in what you made
Because it was made by your belief in it" [33]

How can communication occur when everything that is ever-changing continues to mean different things to each individual? When meaning is established by the accepting of shared symbols that egos can understand you have an ego alliance of division, differences.[34] The clash of bodies (war) becomes justifiable with the ego's defense of these shared differences as truth. However, meaning need not be sacrificed. Meaning can be established and shared by you and your client through any symbol of power that allows you both a shared experience of peace. This is the only value any symbol has.

The Heart of Every Problem

It would be mistaken to give the impression that the five senses are worthless or bad. The senses are appropriately useful and necessary for the body's functioning in a world of change. However, mind has unknowingly hijacked and sabotaged the body and the senses for its own purpose. It uses the experience of the senses to prove to itself that it is subject to and therefore limited by the body it unknowingly made. So, you reel from and become tolerant to the experience of an intoxication you can't understand. While you try to make

---

[33] A Course In Miracles.
[34] The reflection of separation.

sense out of the experience of your confusion, you use the only tool that seems to be available to you; the body that the mind uses to deceive itself. Only chaos and fear could result from this self-deception. That is why your experience of guilt, anger and despair are reoccurring.

To not know is to think
To think is to experience the senses
Knowing is beyond the experience of the senses

At one time you knew, but you do not remember this. You say "I know" all the time, but all you are doing is perceiving . . . all the time! Mind has taken over the use of the body's senses for itself, with the belief that it is subject to the body's external reality of change. In other words, mind perceives that it is a body that it is not. This is evident if you believe pain, fear, anger, guilt, hunger, sacrifice, sorrow and death are real. However, the experience of change does not belong to mind, but to a body of sensation and perception. Mind does not grasp this self-deception because it is preoccupied with defending the experience of the body's senses as a witness to an ephemeral reality as its home. To think other wise is a threat to the ego's existence, and this, the ego cannot tolerate. However, the fact of the matter is;

You may think you desire what you see
But in the beginning you saw what you first desired

A mind that confuses effects[35] as cause does not realize

---

[35] The world you experience as ever-changing.

the extent of its self-deception.[36] You were not "thrown" into this world through birth.[37] Your mind made a world of space and time in order to project a body image! This projection is a substitute for your relationship with Source. This confusion is the source of all sickness.

Misuse of Power

> *"Yeah we're playing those mind games forever*
> *Projecting our images in space and in time"*

Mind Games
John Lennon

You are the power of your creation. A mind that perceives itself as separated from its Source of power feels vulnerable to attack, pain and corruption. In an attempt to find safety from its own confusion, the power of your mind projected an image into space and time, manifested as an ephemeral vehicle you call your body. However, the body's nature is change and therefore incapable of providing a lasting experience of peace and contentment. The separated mind fails to find the safety it desires and finds instead the pain and corruption that all bodies feel.

---

[36] "A human being falsely identifies himself with his physical form because the life currents from the soul are breathed-conveyed into the flesh with such intense power that man mistakes the effect for a cause, and idolatrously imagines the body to have life of its own." Paramahansa Yogananda from Autobiography of a Yogi; P472

[37] As noted by Martin Heidegger's existential philosophy, the only conclusion a *subjective individual* could come to in the light of an existence in which everything is ever-changing is that, "what is" would be a decision to make movement and noise a meaningful choice to one's self.

Only if you believe in a body as your identity
Can you experience being alone, hurt, angry and afraid

Though you experience pain and corruption because of your identification with a body, you feel the need to defend it because you believe it will protect you from the very pain and corruption it causes.[38] Your defense of this impossible contradiction is an attack on your ability to have peace of mind.[39] Because you do not see the mind as separate from bodily conditions, you will impose upon the body all the fear that comes from a mind unaware of its Source. The result is emotional and physical stress on the body you seem to be.

When you give the body goals it cannot reach
You experience anger, guilt and fear

Misuse of power is always the disposition of *a frustrated learner* because they are trying to learn an impossible lesson. The body, being a limitation, cannot live up to the demands of a mind confused about itself. It cannot fix mind's problem. Mind's problem is the belief that it is something it is not. However, you are not the temporary body you identify with. The cause of mind's problem still remains as *an error in thought,* a perceived disconnection from Source. The body is merely the effect of mind's problem, not its cause. All your attempts to find meaningful connections through a body-self

---

[38] This is not meant to imply that you should lay down your body against the onslaught of the world. Rather, remember that by justifying the defense of your illusion, you reinforce the primary block to remembering Source. Only fear can result.

[39] You attack your mind unknowingly because you are the maker of the fear you defend against.

idea are in the end futile substitutions.[40] This is why the body is mind's greatest self-deception. Beyond this confusion, Mind is experienced as eternally changeless.

You Experience What You Believe

Through the experience of a body there seems to be an external world. Your belief in a perceived separation from Source is a projection outside of mind. *You seem to be wired to project rather than reflect.* Unknown to you, you project your confusion as a world. You seem to be born, but it is mind's projection of separation. The entire world is in your mind[41] witnessing to division and corruption while striving through a body to find undying connections that can never be. "Till death do we part" ceremonies, funerals, contracts, pledges of honor, ethical, moral and religious absolutes all fall into this category of symbols of power that try to make the temporary absolute.

Mind's search for a place has decided to limit its power "to be" through the five senses. Thus the senses become the means, the measure and therefore the limit of mind's experience for meaning in the ever-changing.[42] What else could mind find in the appearance of the ever-changing but fleeting shadows that come and go?

---

[40]Meaningful connections through relationships can be found, but if they are an end in themselves they become reasons to believe that abandonment, loss and grief are real; psychological symbols of power that delay peace of mind.

[41]*The Way Home; p167-168*

[42]All empirically scientific data is the proof that all empirically scientific data are empirical and scientific. In other words; all empirical and scientific data reflect a paradigm that is self sustaining, not necessarily self revealing.

If you believe that what you believe will save you
Then the truth would be viewed as threatening
to what you believe

All defenses against the truth
are used to defend the body as true

Because you suffer from what you believe you are, you can heal. If you do not believe this is true, then healing must wait for your acceptance of this principle while mediating forms[43] for relief are to be used. Remember, you do not believe what you experience, you experience what you believe.[44] Allowing for any exception to this principle justifies "the victim" as a symbol of power. It limits your perception and thus your ability to learn. You will experience the effects of your belief until you choose to see it differently.

Self Deception as Betrayal

There is no treachery of betrayal except in self-deception!

Because your mind deceives itself for the purpose of identifying as a body it seems as if the body betrays you when it dies. You may not believe this to be true however, to grieve the loss of something or someone that was never yours to possess in the first place is a self-deception that hides your betrayal.

---

[43]The symbols of power you are willing to accept as having healing influence on the body; the placebo effect.

[44]No thought leaves its source. You always experience the anger, guilt and fear you feel towards someone else. You also experience the love you feel towards someone else. Healing relationships are meant to help you remember you are love. In fact, all relationships teach this.

You are constantly busy with the protection, maintenance, accumulation and continuity of a body. What do you decide and do that does not involve the body? EVERYTHING INVOLVES THE BODY!! To "assume" you are a body hides how preoccupied you are with this idol of limitation. It is an idol of limitation because you place all your aspirations of love, success and peace on it. With that you also reap hate, anger, depression, guilt, pain, hurt, loss and fear! And yet, you will die and everything you worked to achieve will be nothing; a memory to someone for a while . . . to be forgotten.[45] It is only dust, and will return to dust. And yet, you will defend it as you, to your death . . . over and over again.[46]

Knowingly or unknowingly, your mind is always with Source. However, as long as you think the body is you, its end will seem to betray you because it, along with everything else you have embellished and invested in, will perish. No one betrays you but yourself, but even this occurs only in a dream of nothingness . . . and this you can change.

Healing as the Changing of Your Mind

There is no miracle in the healing of a body![47] *The miracle is in the changing of your mind about what you think the body is for.* Use the body as an end, as what you think you are and your symbols of healing will work sometimes. However, the effect is *always* temporary as long as healing is directed at a body that returns to dust. When you can look

---

[45] Ecclesiastes 2:16. All throughout the book of Ecclesiastes is the despair of the ephemeral experience.

[46] *The Way Home; p183*

[47] "A sickly body does not indicate that a guru is lacking in divine powers any more than life long health necessarily indicates inner illumination." Autobiography of a Yogi; p204

without deceit where the real problem was conceived as an error in thought, healing becomes potential.

When you can look beyond seeing any body as sick, then the body can be an opportunity to heal the mind. Thus the body finds its proper place as *a means* to remind you as to where true healing is to be found . . . in the changing of your mind.

Summary

No matter what happens, the body is a part of the cycle of dust. So what are you? What is real? What do you hang your beliefs on? Is there objective meaning outside of your mind when the ever-changing means only what you want it to mean?

Teacher, all of your perceived problems originate from the belief that you are something you are not.[48] *The miracle is in the changing of your mind about what you think the body is for.* Your only betrayal is in self-deception.

Only in self-deception do you not see the betrayal of another
As self-deception

A mind that sees the insignificance of the body recognizes all relationships as opportunities to join at the level of Mind. If joining is not invested in at the level of form, the body can no longer be misused as a means to justify attack or loss as real. Without these justifications, your mind is free to heal, to communicate joining because it looks beyond the belief in a separation that holds guilt or a grudge. Be free from all idols of belief so you can freely use them as they are; temporary aids to help you and your client rise above them all together.

---

[48] The illusion of self esteem. *The Way Home; p158-161*

You are not in the body vessel you think you are
I did not say "The spirit you are
resides in the body vessel you are not"
I said "You are not in the body vessel you think you are"

The body is not right or wrong or good or bad. Nor is there a miracle in the healing of a body! Therefore, it is either an end to nothing or a means to heal your mind. In the mean time you dream a dream, sometimes happy and sometimes sad and scary while you wait for your awakening in Source . . . the remembrance of a belonging *from within,* which lies beyond the senses.

The Earth: Your Reflection

The Earth makes no excuses
It makes no apologies
It is what it is

The Earth makes no promises
It makes no guarantees
It does what it does

Introduction

It is easy to believe that what we see we experience. It is much harder to understand that we experience what we first believed. Through the body, the mind seems to experience a world it is born into, to which it must adapt. At times this world may be appreciated as a God given inspiration or grieved as a terrible tragedy. Always at the end is death.

"Earth is my Mother, no other, my sanctuary
But earth is my prison, my grave and my mortuary"

Earth
James Seals

Simply stated, everything is subject to change. There is nothing that is not subject to change. So your investment for security and identity is in what? The world of appearances deceives the mind that wants to be deceived. Have you set yourself up to believe a lie, experienced that lie as validation for the lie's truth, and then resisted looking at the enormity of your self-deception? [49] Your refusal to see the world for what it is keeps you from generalizing that lesson to everything.

There is no place or object that is holy
They are symbolic of something else

This curriculum is about understanding what the world is for. To understand it you must first forgive it your meanings. When you do, you will understand what the world is for . . . it is for forgiveness.

Catastrophe or Blessing?

Everything our mind perceives is a contradiction. This contradiction is evident in all we experience; the awe of a rainbow arcing over the destruction left by a tornado; the wonder of a waterfall as a fire burns out of control in the surrounding forest above; the colorful beauty of the coral reef as a shark snatches its prey over it. Therefore, in order for the mind to maintain its self-deception, it selectively perceives only that which would validate its beliefs and ignores the rest.[50]

The idea that earth occurrences are natural is correct. However, the idea that these occurrences are catastrophes or blessings is incorrect. These observable phenomena demonstrate the way your ephemeral[51] body processes its state of being . . . as continuous randomization of successive approximations. Because the earth is neither good or bad nor right or wrong, when you take your beliefs and judgments out of it, you will see it reflecting something other than what

---

[49]Denial precedes projection and your projection has been on a scale larger than you realize.

[50]Cherry picking.

[51]As short-lived, transient, brief, temporary, momentary, passing, fleeting and therefore, unpredictable.

you inconsistently believed about it. Teachers who choose to instruct through the dance of Mother Earth, can help by reframing so called catastrophes as Mother Earth's process.

"If you understand, things are the way they are
If you do not understand, things are the way they are"

Zen proverb

Trying to Make Sense Out of the Senseless

Trying to make sense out of the senseless is an impossible goal as you use an ephemeral body[52] to find grounding in an ephemeral world. This confusion is the source of all your sickness. The result is mind's vain attempt to make adjustment upon adjustment through a body to find a place of safety, shelter and comfort in an ever-changing world. In its attempt to find a home of comfort and justice it has found many cunning ways to poison the mother and kill the child. It pollutes the body's drinking water and poisons its food, wages "just" wars in the name of "truth" and tries to possess people, places and things. This is comfort and justice? No, it's insanity!

Because the mind is determined to succeed in its self-deception through a body to make a home, it complicates its confusion by legislating its insanity through the need for ethics, law, economics and social conduct. Through all this you think you will find some semblance of order, safety. But what you find is a complication of living that breeds worry and stress. Have you built a world to hide in, feeling victim to its process, not knowing you made it?

Progress

The idea of progress is about changing and advancing

---

[52] Your body is an aspect of Mother Earth.

conditions. The fruit of progress is called the good life, but it never arrives without complication or cost. To live the good life you make adjustments to work, invest, save and build your little kingdom of safety. Invention and innovation as advancing conditions aren't wrong, they are illusion.

Be an environmental or social activist if you want to. Just don't accept the erroneous idea that to be happy is about trying to change the world. Happiness in the world is not about social, spiritual or even environmental evolution for planetary progress. Being happy is a state of mind that comes from within regardless of what is happening in the world. It's about waking up from a dream that thinks the world is true![53]

Pseudo-Synchronicity

The earth does a dance of random successive approximations. Through your need to make the imprecise meaningful, it is tempting to give sacred meaning to earth's events. For example, "There are more hurricanes than normal." Or, "There are more floods, longer droughts, record snowfalls! Is something significant happening?" Perhaps you want to intervene and redirect the earth's energy[54] through a "collective focus of intention and prayer."[55] Or maybe, "in the

---

[53] *The Way Home; p115-119.* The process of change, of becoming, is about the ephemeral. Waking up to what you already are, is about Spirit.

[54] The universe is the miscreation of an idle projected thought. Energy, being a different form of matter is nothing but projected thought.

[55] The Harmonic Convergence is a New Age astrological term applied to a planetary alignment, which occurred on August 16–17, 1987. The timing of the Harmonic Convergence allegedly correlated with the Mayan calendar, with some consideration also given to European and Asian astrological traditions. The chosen dates have the distinction of allegedly marking a planetary alignment with the Sun, Moon and six out of eight planets being "part of the grand trine." The convergence is purported to have "corresponded with a great shift in the earth's energy from warlike to peaceful." It was an opportunity for many to join minds for the purpose of peace.

year 2012,[56] the moon is eclipsing[57] at a sacred portal[58] at 6:66 pm,[59] near the time of an equinox or solstice,[60] which happens to be at a time that nine[61] of the planets may be in our night sky. This must mean something significantly important!" Or else it is a pseudo-synchronicity the ego uses to spiritualize (make sacred) the process of "ashes to ashes, dust to dust."

No matter what's happening *out there*, it's not really happening *out there*. Out there is a reflection of what is happening at the level of your mind. Whether you are talking about disaster or bounty, it is you who try to make the senseless phenomena of random occurrences seem meaningfully real.

Sacred Magic

If you can see that you have been looking for grounding where it cannot be found, you also come to understand how special gatherings of special events for special reasons in

---

[56] The end of the Mayan calendar . . . maybe the end of the world, or the beginning of Armageddon . . . or whatever you like it to mean.

[57] A solar eclipse occurs when the moon passes between the sun and the earth. This symbolizes unification of focus, healing. A lunar eclipse occurs when the moon passes behind the earth so that the earth blocks the sun's rays from striking the moon. This symbolizes polarity, tension.

[58] Doorway, gateway. entrance.

[59] 666 is the symbol for *the mark of the beast* out of revelations 13:18. It means a lot of things to a lot of theologians. If you are trying to prove something, you could use it to make it mean something for you. By the way some manuscripts read 616. Yes, I know there is no such time as 6:66 unless it is secretly symbolic for 7:06 which may be a sign for something else special. Mae West said "1 and 1 is 2; 2 and 2 is 4; and 4 and 4 is 10, if you know how to work it right."

[60] The equinox is when the suns rays directly hit the equator. The solstice is when the earth's tilt is at one extreme or the other. These all represent the markings of the seasons.

[61] The number for completion in numerology.

special circles[62] or special buildings with special people using special rituals with special rocks, incense, feathers and all kinds of other special elements of the earth, performed by very special people, for special healings . . . can be made *sacred*.[63]

Despite ritualizing the ever-changing to make it magical, Mother Earth is the cause of nothing. Therefore, the earth has no effect. It is not sacred. It is nothing because it was made by you without Source and therefore it was made out of fear. Out of fear you select ever-changing people, places and things to be special substitutions to hide behind, from your Source. How you decide what is to be sacred and what is not is incomprehensible. Either it is all sacred or none of it is!

In terms of the ever-changing, you are the cause of a miscreation with no effect. There is nothing special about any of those things. It is simply a sacred magic of belief . . . in nothingness.

What the Earth Really Demonstrates

You believe the world is real because it was made by your belief in it. Your mind is so powerful that it can make a world untrue for you to experience as real. The earth is your projection to hide your guilt . . . and a very good job you did . . . to hide your guilt from your conscious mind. The catastrophe you see in your world is the catastrophe you refuse to see originating in your mind . . . the belief you can separate from the Source of your creation. What else could result from this self-deception but an attempt to bury a

---

[62]Or "special places" such as spiritual vortexes where energy or life forces seem to enter the earth from beyond.
[63]*The Way Home; p149-151*

perpetual separation anxiety to avoid punishment and grief. Yet, you experience anxiety, pain and grief anyway.

What does the Earth teach? It teaches the cycle of impermanence. Birth to death to birth to death is constantly demonstrated through the changes of the seasons. What else could it teach but the obvious? And the body you think you are is but an aspect of the obvious.

> *"Saving up your money for a rainy day*
> *Giving all your clothes to charity*
> *Last night the wife said, 'Oh boy when you're dead*
> *You don't take nothing with you but your soul' . . . Think!"*

Ballad of John and Yoko
Lennon & McCartney

Your insane interpretation of Mother Earth demonstrates that you are a wanderer lost in a world you made by your belief in it. When it is time for you to release the symbols you made sacred to enslave you, you will be able to use them to show you the way out. Your journey back to Source will happen when you see that you are more than the dust of sacred nothingness you call Mother Earth.

Raise to Question

Teachers of the dance, raise to question the way of nature, the circle of life and death, the shedding of a blood sacrifice for absolution. The temptation to explain your projection of the ephemeral by mystifying it as "God's beautiful creation" only makes the dust of change an untouchable spiritual idol for the sleepy mind that made it a dream. To make earth events as "The Will of God" spiritualizes distractions your ego will vigorously defend. This is because all appearances of nature are the illusion of "something significant" the ego hides behind for its survival. God is not the creator of uncertainty, change, pleasure, pain and death. We are!! Stop the madness of ascribing causes to a god that God does not claim![64] Rather, enjoy what you seem to come upon. Cry if it seems to be the need of the moment. Be a passerby by making your journey through the dream, an adventure. *Just don't invest in its process as something sacred.*

Acceptance

You experience self-deception on a daily basis and you would be able to see it if you looked honestly at it. Everything that has been built and will be built will dissolve into sacred nothingness. Acceptance is yielding to the recognition that you made a world unreal to truth and believe it.

The world does nothing to you
You only thought it did
Nor do you do anything to the world
Because you were mistaken about what it is [65]

The earth is neither good or bad, nor right or wrong. When you take your beliefs and judgments out of it, you can use the earth as a means to reflect something other than your projected guilt that defends a body-self idea to be born to struggle, achieve, experience pleasure and pain and then die again and again. Allow the symbol of Mother to teach you

---

[64] *The Way Home; p139-144*
[65] A Course in Miracles; Manual for Teachers; paraphrase, p18

that you are more than the sacred dust of the earth. Allow your projection to reflect your innocence. But first you must understand where innocence comes from.

Summary

Your mind is so powerful that it can make a world untrue for you to experience as real. You do not believe this because you use the power of your mind to deny the power it is. Give it back to the Spirit of Truth so your mind can be used to remedy your dream of self-deception.

Teachers of the dance, you may think earth history, personal history, culture, sociology, etc., plays a part in defining what you are. However, they are an effect of not knowing what you are. They reinforce to teach you what you are not! Do not use symbols and rituals of the earth to enslave the mind to the idea that the grave is your end, for they are an end to nothing. Rather, allow those earth symbols and rituals the opportunity to remind you that what you are lives beyond the dust of time. Then you will know how to appreciate the earth for what it is.

The world you made was made out of an error of thought. Don't think you can find any solution in the world. It was made so you could not escape from your problems. You may think you have choices that make a difference but they are all choices that keep you invested in the world. Your refusal to see the world for what it is keeps you from the only meaningful choice you can make!

Beyond the world you made is the real world. To remember it is to want only to understand all things the way they are. Your perception of it must change before it is to be understood. Then you will understand that the reason for the world is to forgive it the beliefs you have given it. Until then, you seem to be a wanderer . . . moving through time and space. Therefore, enjoy the rainbow, the water fall, and the sunset. Dance around the fire that symbolizes your purification, your initiation to your next step. Feel the exhilarating power of a thunderstorm. And when you remember them to be but reflections of your abundance in Source, they will be a means to help you awaken. Understand gratitude and you will find contentment through change.

> *"So keep on playing those mind games together*
> *Doing the ritual, dance in the sun"*

Mind Games
John Lennon

The Concept of Magic

"We all been playing those mind games forever
Some kind of druid dude, lifting the veil
Doing the mind guerrilla
Some call it magic, the search for the grail"

Mind Games
John Lennon

Introduction

Magic is placing reliance on you alone. It is the manipulation of the external; people and things for desired outcomes. It is a substitution for your reliance and direction in Source. It is a substitution for true assistance. True assistance is your ability to help your client reframe substitutions that limit inner peace.

Mediating Forms

Practices such as physical healings, incantations, rituals with religious or pagan symbols, taking an aspirin for a headache have outcomes that seem to be a cause of healing. However, they are mediating forms (substitutions) for what the mind seems unable to do for itself. Healing directly through the mind becomes impossible when you fear the thoughts you harbor. The primary thought you harbor is the belief you can oppose the will of your Source and succeed. So you look out on a world you made out of fear to hide from your fear, seeking aids for healing in forms that do not seem to threaten you. It is your desire for healing that allows these aids to be mediating forms you can accept.

Resistance to Heal

Any form of healing that is a focus outside of your mind may have temporary results. You know the results are temporary when you engage in a constant search for healing resolve. Your problem seems to be one thing this day and another thing the next day. Why is your search endless? It is endless because the world of form is an outcome removed from the solution; the mind that thought the problem in the first place. Your savior seems to appear outside of you for relief because you cannot bring the problem to the cause. The only place where real healing occurs is at the level of changing your mind, not in your manipulation of the world of form. Manipulation of form for results is what magic is. It is any substitution for your reliance on Source.

How can you correct the error if you do not realize
That you are under the spell of your own magic?

To tell you that none of your problems are real would be a laughable outrage to those who believe in them. However, it is your thoughts that cause the problems you experience. *You think* you are affected by the world. But it is a world you projected.

The concept of magic is a placebo effect to the one who needs a savior outside of Source. It provides temporary relief but never release. Though placebo effects of all kinds demonstrate *mind over matter*, your mind is too divided and resistant to be able to generalize that truth to everything. Healing must wait for your readiness to look within to the power of your mind, for that is where lasting healing resides.

Summary

To look for a savior outside of Source is a delay tactic of placing reliance on you alone. It is the manipulation of form for desired outcomes that delays your remembering of where your journey lies. It is smoke and mirror magic that tricks you into believing the world you dream is real.

Teacher, because sickness is of the mind, so is healing. If your client is afraid to heal, mediating forms the mind can accept will appear. These forms of relief your client presents are not right or wrong or good or bad. They are tangible forms for relief your client can accept at the time. *True assistance* is using the mediating forms your client presents as opportunities to go beyond what those forms represent.

Healer, though they are temporary, you can use these aids as steps towards your clients awakening. To be able to use their symbols is the communication of joining with them.

Shaman, allow no symbol or form of ritual to be a delay to you and your student's journey home.

Magician, remove the smoke and mirror from your eyes so you can help the student see what is behind the curtain.[66] The ever-changing is but a veil to delay your reminder of where the changeless awaits your remembrance.

---

[66]Not unlike the curtain which the Wizard of Oz hid behind while the five travelers interacted with a projection . . . until Toto sniffed it out.

The Astral Realm

Space and time cannot limit the mind
That lets the body go

Realms of Consciousness

Dreaming Beyond the Body

Realms of Consciousness

Introduction

Do not deny the mind its ability to free itself from body identification and you will empower its potential to go beyond any idea of space and time.

In truth, different realms of consciousness are unknown to the mind free of all limiting thoughts. Limitation is not experienced by a free mind. A free mind knows [67] and is known by Source. Within Source there are no realms of consciousness. However, a mind that believes in thoughts that limit its experience of being, projects an image (by thought) of an ephemeral body into space and time. Such misuse of mind's power results in the experience of seemingly different levels of awareness. These experiences of different levels are called by many names depending on the discipline of study. They are summarized here as realms of consciousness.

Realms of Consciousness

The ephemeral realm is currently your primary realm of consciousness. It is the realm of shifting and fleeting forms, dependent on the appearance of space and time. It is the home of the body you think you are. In it, empires come and empires go.

The astral realm is a thought projection of self through space.[68] Time is not a factor in this experience of consciousness because your mind does not identify with a body-self idea that binds itself to birth and death.

---

[67]To know and to believe are two different things. To believe involves doubt and the need to defend. To know involves nothing of the sort.

[68]Some consider an out-of-body experience as the self-deception of a hallucination. That would be correct, and so is your ephemeral experience of a body.

The spiritual realm is your inner place of Being in Source. It is your identity beyond your experience of the ephemeral and astral realms. To some it means heaven. Here, there is no duality of an inner or outer world because there is no outer world.

Time

Though time travel is greatly sensationalized, Mind does not travel in time. It can remember the experience of a yesterday as if it was there, but that is something different than time travel.[69]

Time is an illusion of linear dimension. It is always a present thought experience of a memory. Any recollected memory (the past) can be the anticipation of tomorrow. The anticipation of a future based on a remembered thought seems to make time a real life idea. Yet, no matter how you think about it, whether it is a thought gone by or the anticipation of a future possibility, *each and every experience you have is always in the present moment.* Self-deception is the experience of a past tense that anticipates a future tense, blocking your awareness of the only tense there is . . . the present. Because you are not always aware of the present tense does not mean it is not there. That is why time is an illusion of linear dimension.

Space

Space is the idea of an image projected by thought, away from Source, into mind's conscious void. Void is the emptiness of nothing. A self concept based upon a physical body is merely an image of mind's projection nowhere.

Your mind is experiencing its beliefs as if they are out

---

[69]The experience of recollection.

there. But there is no out there. This seems incomprehensible to the mind given over to the denial of its projections . . . the experience of its beliefs as if it were outside of mind.

It is Mind's nature to create. However, instead of creating like itself, mind projects the error of separation. The power of your mind to divide, multiplies into ever-changing forms. Void becomes identified as quantitative space when objects are measured with distance between them. Nothing is stationary on this rotating, revolving orb we call earth. Because all objects move, measurements between objects are in constant flux. Space becomes the relationship of ever-shifting distances between the senses of your body and all other objects.

The Projecting of a "self image"

The projection of a self image as a body is always *away from* the awareness of Source.[70] It is looking out. This projection into space (mind's void) coupled with the marking of thought experiences in time is the making of the wanderer, seemingly drifting through realms of consciousness. This is all done in the world of a confused mind as it looks away from Source and onto the making of its own experience in a void of nothingness

When mind frees itself from the idea of body identification, astral mobility becomes potential. This is possible because it is your natural inclination to be free of limiting thoughts of body identity. Your ability to suspend self-imposed limits finds its potential in the present. To move beyond these limits is not difficult when you understand that your mind already

---

[70]Because denial always precedes projection, you are not aware of what you have done.

waits for your remembrance at the end of time, the door of eternity.

Truth will teach time to give way to Eternity

That you can project a thought of yourself beyond the body anywhere into space is nothing. This is because you unknowingly have already done this through an ephemeral body! That you realize body identification as a limiting concept of time and space is everything.

Signposts

The astral realm is the idea of a self-image projected through space. Many remember the experience of being somewhere outside of their body. A common example would be a sense of floating at the ceiling looking down at your sleeping body. The astral realm is different from *recollection*.[71] Recollection is a present memory of a past body experience. Many have had the experience of remembering historical situations of a past life.

The experience of the astral has nothing to do with the five senses of the perceived world because it is a projection out of the ephemeral realm of the body's senses. Unlike recollection, the experience of the astral realm only occurs in your present tense of time.

The experience of the astral realm allows your mind room to put your physical body in a different perspective. It is a realization that you are more than the experiences of your ephemeral body. With the projection of an experience outside of your body, you come to realize there is something about you that is not born to die. You may have a "wow"

---

[71]This has also been called regression.

experience of freedom from your limiting beliefs about you as a body. However, as a projection, it is still removed from your Source of knowing.

Teachers of Truth

Teachers of truth, remind your students that the astral realm is just another realm of *temporary* consciousness, a substitute experience for remembering Source. Don't get caught up in the glamour of the astral. That would make it another form of delay.

Everything outside of your center has a temporary purpose; to bring you back to Source. That is the only value it has. Don't use this experience as delay. And as you move through space and time . . . in the realms of your mind . . . enjoy the ride.

Summary

Looking outside of Source, through the projection of an image into a void of nothingness, realms of consciousness seem to exist. Projections are recognized in relation to external orientation. Most have gotten lost in the cycle of the ephemeral. Some have gotten lost in the glamour of the astral. Your astral projections witness to the fact that you are more than a body. They also witness to the fact that you can deceive yourself on a grand scale and not know it. Your astral projections are not true either. Keep moving!

Dreaming Beyond the Body

Introduction

It is likely that everyone has had out of body experiences. This is a very natural phenomenon that many do not recognize. The problem is one of misinterpreting your experiences with preconceived notions.

A Relaxed Mind

The frantic world of a racing mind does not know how to rest. It is preoccupied with the needs and desires of a body. As a result, exhaustion, stress, worry, illness and various other forms of escape occupy the mind. This scenario shows how out of control a thinking mind is.

A relaxed mind is able to suspend its beliefs as being an individual body identity. This is the condition necessary for an out of body experience to occur. Because undisciplined thinking is not an aspect of a relaxed mind, the most common time to actualize your potential for an out of body experience is when you lay your body down to sleep.[72] In the twilight between wake and sleep the mind relaxes its fixed beliefs about everything. Mind drifts into a relaxed state when occurring thoughts are not given immediate consideration.

Parameters of Experience

When you sleep, thoughts that limit experience are relaxed. Wandering thoughts are randomly woven together into an experience of the absurd. When we wake and remember them, they are labeled as dreams; and rightfully so. They are merely random thoughts with no thematic connection. Dream

---

[72]This can also happen through meditation.

interpretation works when you find a theme that can tie together and transcend the absurdity of those thoughts. It is the theme that brings meaning to the absurd.

Other experiences also occur when your mind is in a relaxed state of suspended limitation. These experiences have also been readily labeled without question as dreams. Mind's ability to experience astral travel and past body recollections are easily mislabeled as an experience of dreaming, though the experience was not an absurd story line. In other words what you might assume to be a dream of the absurd was actually astral travel or a past life recollection.

The determination of the mind to deceive itself into believing it is a body only allows for the five senses as parameters of experience. These parameters must be maintained at all cost because they defend the lie your mind has chosen for its security. The lie is, "You are not the eternal creation of your Source. You are a body begotten of other bodies to beget other bodies." To seriously question this is to set your whole kingdom of body investment upside down. *All defenses against Truth are used to defend the body as real.*

If you believe what you believe will save you
The Truth will be threatening to what you believe

Past life recollection and astral mobility need no theme. They are experiences of opportunity that can remind you that you are more than a body . . . when you do not discount them as "just another dream." Though they are dreams, they both demonstrate that you are more than the body you think you are.

Mind's Propensity for Self-Deception

Fear is a helpful indication that you have lied to yourself

Because you have erroneously identified yourself as a body, any experience to the contrary can be fearfully interpreted. To protect itself from the fear of being mistaken, your mind will need to discount the paranormal if it cannot be explained within the parameters of the five senses. The ego's defense is to keep the experience in question out of the question. It prevents your parameters of interpretation from being scrutinized. For example, either your paranormal experiences should be denied relevance because they cannot be empirically proven or you can elevate these experiences to the statutes of a mystery. Either way they have been put out of reach for you to use as a means to free you. If you would use your "out of the box" experiences to acknowledge the power of your mind, you would see your self-deception. You are not the body you think you are. The ego cannot accept this because to expose the fallacy of your world view would threaten the ego's survival.

Your defense of any interpretation to protect you from fear Is the cause of your fear

It is paramount for you to recognize your mind's propensity to deceive itself with assumptions and then to experience those assumptions as self validating truth.

Summary

Within your dream of separation are dreams you dream. There are dreams of the absurd. There are dreams of astral mobility and past life recollections. Sensitize your mind to be willing to remember its natural expression of freedom. Begin to recognize your astral experiences as opportunities that teach you that you are something other than a body.

If space is merely the relationship between objects of movement projected by your mind into the void of consciousness, you will find your Self everywhere. If time is merely a present thought experience recollected and anticipated, you will find your Self everywhere . . . now.

Dreams

As you wish . . .
There will be lots of messages in dreams
Just as there are lots of dreams in messages
It is within the power of your mind to get lost in them
. . . And not know it . . .

The Art of Dream Interpretation

Another Dream State

The Art of Dream Interpretation

Dream interpretation can be a creative endeavor
When it is used to go beyond the temptation
To limit the dream's symbolic meaning . . .
. . . To the ephemeral experience

Introduction

Emphasis is often placed on dreams as symbols of hidden personal meanings. This assumption breeds opportunities for misunderstanding and misuse. Dreams can be used as a creative process for inner healing when they are not used to testify to experiences of self-deception. Due to confusion regarding dreams and other experiences mistakenly associated as dreams, clarification is needed.

What is a Dream?

When you are sleeping, a dream is not a related set of circumstances and events. Rather, it is unrelated pieces of projected impressions from memory retained in your unconscious mind. Some of these impressions are stored in the unconscious in order to forget unpleasant experiences. Others are stored over the forgetfulness of times gone by.

As your body sleeps, your mind's self-imposed limitations are relaxed. The organizational patterns of memory storage also relax. The stage is set for images from your body memories to loosely flow together in no particular order out of the unconscious. These images, randomly chosen and unrelated, come together to form a series of picture impressions in your sleeping mind.[73] The random recall of these impres-

---

[73]Actually, the mind never sleeps but consciousness is temporarily laid to rest.

sions explains the absurdity of your dream experience. When you awaken with strong feelings from some of these impressions, the temptation is to desire a personally meaningful understanding. Too often, an interpreted story line is imposed on these random impressions in an attempt to give meaningful relief to your emotional response. Your range of intense responses associated with these random impressions occurs because of your mind's identification and investment in an ephemeral body. Your discomfort is a superficial effect on the conscious level. It masks your making of an unconscious level to hide your fear of an infinite mind that has limited itself to the identity of a dream of birth, pain and death. This error allows for all kinds of misinterpretations of what your sleep dreams symbolize.

Your clients will come to you seeking a meaningful resolve to their intense reactions to these random impressions. To help them understand their sleeping dream, the interpretation of symbolic meaning[74] becomes important.

The Making of the Dream

My spirit does not know of limitation
If I believe in limitation, I deny my reality in Spirit
This is called dreaming

Because the idea that the limitless can limit itself is a contradiction of thought, your mind enters into conflict. This conflict produces what is called a dream state. In this state, the

---

[74]People don't necessarily believe the sleeping dream is true as much as what they think it represents; i.e., if I dream of having an affair, it's not that I think it will happen as much as it might symbolize an unhappy relationship.

power of your mind projects its thoughts of conflict to be fearfully real. Whether you seem to be awake or asleep, these thoughts become everything you experience through the life of a body.

You made the dream but think the dream made you
That's what makes your life in a body a dream

Teacher, how can you see another's script for what it is when you are busily trying to teach the impossible; how to make your awake dream real?

Dream's Meaning

Your mind has the ability to bring absurd pictures together, and is often eager to interpret these picture relationships as something meaningful. For example, you can easily interpret a sleeping dream of falling as being out of control; a dream in which you are unable to move or call for help may seem to signify vulnerability; the dream of failing a test may be construed as feelings of inadequacy or fear of failure. However, the importance of any dream is *only* in the importance the dreamer gives it.

The meaning of any dream lies with
your decision about the dream
Not within the dream itself

Dream Weaver, how can you assist in your client's interpretation of their dream if you are busy trying to make your dream real? Help your client to interpret symbols that look beyond the dream.

What Dreams Teach

Everyone has at some point in their life believed that a dream was real . . . until they woke up thinking with relief "Oh thank goodness, it was just a dream!" What seemed so real asleep can be seen as nonsense when awake. Therefore, the most important thing to remember about dreams is;

Dreams teach that you can believe the impossible

You seemed to experience *the impossible* as real, yet were deceived. Perhaps your wakened state is another 'dream' of self-deception? Consider how you were able to experience a world in your sleep dream where none exists. Then remember, dreams teach that you can believe the impossible. While all your sleeping dreams seem to reflect the world of your waking state, your waking state is but a dream in another form. Whether you sleep or not, your life in a body is but a dream!

Row row row your boat gently down the stream
Merrily merrily merrily merrily
Life is but a dream

You do not believe what you experience, you experience what you believe. Your experience is a deception that overwhelms your ability to remember what you once knew before believing became a substitute for knowing.[75] You seem to believe what you experience. And what you experience, you believe to be true. *You made the dream but think the dream made you.* Your self-deception is almost complete![76]

---

[75]*The Way Home; p125*
[76]The intellect of thinking is an enormous symbol of power. It needs the humility of a proper perspective.

The Power of Dreams

As long as you wander unknowingly in a place not your home, the desire remains strong to make meaningful that which is not your own. This is the power of your dream to deceive. The adept dream interpreter will be aware of the dreamer's tendency to desire a story that is not so. The interpreter will be able to help the dreamer reinterpret any dream in a way that transcends the dream. Because dreams teach that you can believe the impossible, any interpretation that helps you approach the awakening from your dream lends the dream the power you need to facilitate healing.

Dream Interpreter, one who has dreams of dying will turn all symbols into fear until he understands that all symbols are open to reframing. What was once interpreted as fear of death can be symbolically interpreted as that which has to die so something new can take its place. This reframing transfers symbols of resistance into symbols of assistance.

Summary

All symbols of the ephemeral are to be understood within a larger context . . . from outside of the dream altogether. Dream Interpreter, in order to be able to interpret all dreams for healing purposes, remain aware of your propensity to want to believe that your awake dreams are true. The interpretations of your client's sleep dreams are no different than the interpretation of your own awake dreams because . . . they are both dreams.

What symbol of power
used to hold the dreamer within the conflict of his mind
can save him from the lostness of his dream?[77]

---

[77]*The Way Home; p124*

The adept dream interpreter is able to recognize and clarify symbols of the dream so the client can move towards awakening from the dream altogether. *The fact that all dreams teach that you can believe the impossible is the only value any dream interpretation has.*

Sleepy dreamer, lost under the enchantment of your own spell, mediate the meanings of your own making. All your dreams have but one message to teach you; what you made, you mistook as real. Your restless sleep dreams and restless awake dreams is a stirring for you to awaken from the dream altogether.

Dream Weaver, just for you, teach your client that the dream they react to is of their making. When you remind them that the dream points to a state of mind beyond the dream itself, you help yourself to wake up.

Another Dream State

There is a realm other than what you experience
through the five senses
If you allow your mind room for it

Introduction

Experiencing life through the body's senses is like inter-preting objects through the distortion of a glass of water. If you do not recognize your body as a means for distortion, you will use it as a tool to try and make sense out of the ever-changing world. To try and make sense through a distortion that is not you is a disability which prevents you from remembering what you really are. To forget what you are is to experience a dream state and not know it.

Just because your body seems to be awake
does not mean you are

Whatever dream state you seem to be in is irrelevant if your distortion does not allow you to recognize your natural state. That is why your sleep dreams provide just as much opportunity to awaken as your awake dreams.

Until you awaken to your natural Self
Everything is dream interpretation

The Illusion of Disembodied Spirits

Because confusion exists in the mind, disorientation easily occurs to some at the time of their body's death, resulting in a state of existence we call ghosts. Ghosts are spirits who resist separating their identity from their physical body.[78] They roam in a different form of dreaming, through familiar scenes, thinking they are still associated with a body. All things are possible to the mind that dreams.

It is through the limiting experience of a body that time (birth and death) and space (place) seem to have meaning. When your body dies you are released to remember these two to be an illusion, unless you resist mental separation from your body. Though ghosts believe themselves to be in a body, they are free to roam beyond the illusive limits of space and time. That is why some places have an extensive history of being haunted. They frequent places they knew as bodies or "haunt" the place of their exit from their body. To the mind limited to the illusion of a body in space and time, the antics of a ghost can be easily interpreted as prankish. And because it is an experience beyond the predictable limits of the five senses, it can easily be distorted as fearful. Because ghosts are unaware of being "out of body," their need is to wake up.

Unfinished Business

It is believed that ghosts linger because of unfinished business. It is also easy to think ghosts linger because they have interpreted body death departures as fearfully traumatic. And fearfully traumatic they may have seemed to the one who resisted death. However, whether it is fearfully traumatic or not, any unfinished business will bring you back. Unfinished business merely reflects work to be done to awaken from the dream.

---

[78]Ghosts are aspects of One Mind clinging to their disembodied projection of a body consciousness. Angels are messengers of One Mind appearing as projected images in the mind of the dreamer.

Ghosts are those who do not realize their elusive body died. They are acting as if it is still alive. In self-deception, they are dreaming their life through another dream state. It is continued dreaming that withholds the recognition that the body they once projected is gone. They remain to finish business.

Summary

The mind that is confused about itself, dreams the impossible. A ghost state reflects mind's propensity to dream the impossible. However, whatever you dream is not relevant. What matters is awakening from the dream altogether.

Attempting to chase a ghost out of a familiar haunt without helping to facilitate their awakening achieves nothing. Be patient when they fear the call to heal. To help a confused spirit move beyond their dream involves getting their attention. Any disembodied spirit's natural desire to awaken will eventually lead them back into the cycle of healing.

Déjà Vu

*When you reach the end
you will find yourself at the beginning
In between the two are experiences
you have already traveled*

Introduction

There is nothing mystical about a déjà vu experience unless you think an experience other than your current body orientation is something mystical.

A Fleeting Remembrance

In a relaxed state, mind has the potential to recall experiences from past body identities. It also has the ability to project into mind's space. The duration of any of these experiences involves your ability to suspend your limiting thoughts about your current body identity.

A déjà vu experience is a fleeting remembrance of a past experience triggered by a present stimulus / encounter. It is as if "I've lived this moment before, exactly as it's happening now." It's like a memory and a moment in one. It's illustrated in the expressions "I've done this before," or "I've been here before," or "I feel like I've met you before." As you try to savor the experience, it fades. Now only its fleeting memory remains.

Summary

Any experience you can identify as something beyond the experience of the five senses is a breakthrough. It reminds you that there is a disposition of being beyond the limits your mind has placed on your body. Teacher, do not get side tracked interpreting the *"wows"* of what those experiences might mean.

Cultures of Lore

The one thing history teaches
Is that we don't learn from it

Introduction

Don't believe that certain cultures of the past were any more advanced or special than the age of today!

Romanticizing the Past

One may romanticize past cultures as having had more information about the wholeness of healing. However, if this information had been personalized into the core of the people, if they had lived the information they possessed, they never would have lost it! History indicates that the Atlanteans, Mayans, Lemurians, Tibetans, Druids, etc., lost sight of their inheritance. Today, we are witnesses to the loss of what true healing is about.

"The world we know is thinking with a hand-me-down brain
Insane because it bubbles like the rain causes puddles
We can't walk so we must sit
While the world goes on and on
Thinking with a hand me down brain"

Hand Me Down Shoe
James Seals / Dash Crofts

Do we make cultures and people of other times something different and therefore special? It is tempting to idolize certain people and attribute advanced characteristics to them and therefore make history seem real.

The Illusion of Progress

Depending on your perspective, you can see in many ways how human kind is evolving. Yet, the lesson that history teaches is that we don't learn from it.

It is erroneous to measure an evolution of awareness out of economic and technical achievements. These achievements have also been used to find better ways to accumulate the illusion of power and kill bodies. And the ability to proselytize the illusion of freedom and democracy easily hides the human condition of greed. Without the power you are in Source, "all your mind can do is seemingly divide and subdivide and then attempt to glorify the results."[79]

On an unconscious level there is a desire to remember Source. However, this desire is trumped by a desire to ingratiate your body. Because all bodies are born out of guilt, they desire substitutions that deny the Truth of your reality in Source. Denial breeds fear. Though you have made amazing technical and scientific progress to save and comfort bodies, human kind continues to use this technology to find clever ways to steal and kill.

The illusion of external change as advancement has nothing to do with an evolution of global awareness. Your condition of guilt is played out in whatever form is presented. That is why the one thing history teaches us is that we don't learn from it.

Dissemination of Information

In the world of change, change has always been the norm while awareness remains with a few. I do not deny that there is a dissemination of logic on a global level that has never been

---

[79]The Disappearance of the Universe, Gary R. Renard; p126

since the dawn of this civilization. So is there a dissemination of misinformation for the mind that wants to be deceived.

Logic teaches that;
1. When you try to be something you are not, you will feel vulnerable.
2. From this vulnerable position is your making of fear.
3. Your defense of this vulnerability is an attack on the Truth of what You really are.
4. Because you attack the Truth of what You are through all your substitutions to deny this Truth, you always attack yourself first.

The mind that sees the error of their logic does not find this hard to understand. They see progress as what it is, smoke and mirror substitutions from waking up.

Summary
Because there never was a past and there will never be a future, our focus need not be about the history of idolized civilizations. Our focus is better served on the opportunity to forgive now.

Let not the illusion of external change seen as progress, deceive you into believing in an evolution of awareness. It is not about evolving, it is about waking up. No matter what the substitutions of progress look like, you are born to undo the guilt you assume. There may be more people becoming aware, yet it is you alone that is the student of awareness as you teach your clients to wake up . . . for no one can awaken you but yourself.

We live to wander to die
Until we remember where our inheritance lies

Karma

What you see is what you get
What you get is your own mind set

Karma and Your Destiny

Where is Karma?

The Lash of the Dragon's Tail

Karma and Your Destiny

Because no thought leaves its source
You will experience and act out the thoughts you think

Introduction

What you think, you will act out. What you act out is your destiny. Karma is neither good nor bad. It's not "payback" for bad behavior or "reward" for good behavior. It is the destiny you act out dependent upon what you think. It is your reflection of shadows interpreted as your world. It is the projection of the dance you do in your mind. It is your effect.

Karma crosses apparent lifetimes as your collection of yesterday's unresolved memories. You are unaware that you make a destiny that is dependent upon what you think because;

Denial always precedes projection

The Fact of the Matter

Whether you believe in karma or not is irrelevant to the fact that every thought you entertain evokes a response. Said in other ways, "He who sows the wind reaps the whirlwind" [80] or "Do not judge lest you be judged. For in the way you judge, you will be judged; and by your standard of measure, it will be measured to you." [81] or "Instant karma's gonna' get you."[82] In other words;

---

[80] A loose translation of Proverbs 22:8, Hosea 8:7, also James 3:18 & Galatians 6: 7-8.
[81] Matthew 7: 1-3.
[82] John Lennon

Because no thought leaves its source
Every wish finds its fulfillment in the mind that thought it

Karma is the effect of what you think . . . and what you think you will experience *as if* it is real.

Maker of Fate

Because you make your own fate, you are the victim or savior of the fate you make. When you allow yourself to become aware of this fact, you can begin the work that cancels your karmic debt. You begin the work when you realize that the problem is in the same place as the solution . . . with you!

No matter what countless forms your life seems to take or appears to be, it's all karmic. However, because *complexity of form does not imply complexity of content,* there is a simple solution. This solution goes back to the mind that thought it could get rid of the thoughts it does not like, through projection. You can change your mind about anything. Until you decide differently, you are the self-made victim unknowingly collecting and safeguarding your own fate, to play over and over again in countless forms.[83]

Karma as an Instant Effect

"Return to sender, address unknown
No such number, no such zone"

Otis Blackwell / Winfield Scott

The letters that show up in your mailbox arrive because they have your address on them. Someone knew how to

---

[83]This is where blame gets its power to thrive. "What happens to me is your fault" is the ego's way of keeping you in a karmic loop of being a victim of your own thoughts . . . unaware that there is a way to interrupt it.

reach you. The events in your life are like those letters, with one significant difference. Without realizing it, you have mailed them to yourself. Check the handwriting on the envelope. If you look closely, you can tell that it is your own. Open it. Read it. Drink it all in. Take this message to heart. When you see that *in every circumstance* you are the cause of how you see what you think you understand, then you will see the way to break your karmic cycle.[84]

What you make real in your mind is real to you. What you do not understand is that what is real to you, you first made real in your mind. Every thought has an immediate effect. You always experience *instantly* the thoughts you choose to entertain about everything.

> *The thoughts you have about another*
> *Is always a gift to you first*
> *What kind of gift are you giving?*

Be conscious of the thoughts you are thinking because you might want to change them. When you make what you do not like, you can either recognize you made it so you can change your mind about it, or you can try to avoid it by projecting it away.

Despite your attempts to throw away a problem *you made* by trying to hang it on someone else, it remains in your mind. As a subtle irritation, grievance or sadness, it remains as a projection on some unsuspecting wanderer you think you know. Because you made it, you cannot give it away through blame, ignorance or any cause you devise. You can hide it to play it again at a later time in the form of a different problem

---

[84]Because karma is neither good nor bad, you can also send yourself messages of hope, peace and love.

or you can give it to forgiveness as a mindless cause of nothingness. There is no escape from karma except through forgiveness. Forgiveness is the only function meaningful in time because it is the only function you can use to collapse time.

Instant Karma at Work

Whatever I do to you, I do to myself
What can I do so I won't suffer?

If your goal is peace of mind, to shorten or collapse time brings you closer to your goal. It is not your actions that cause you conflict. They are an effect. It is mind's interpretation of those actions that cause your internal conflicts. It is your mind alone that assigns value (meaning) to anything. If you do not know this to be true, you will believe truth is to be found outside of you.[85] Only self-righteous interpretations of behavior follow from this belief. You will *always* be found guilty of violating the same standard you set for another.[86] This is karma at work.

Every mind in conflict is a mind living within
the conflict of its own decision

The threat you feel is not outside of you. It is projected away to be perceived as outside of you. It is a consequence of not recognizing the battle you perceive as going on in the

---

[85]This is what *sacred texts, sacred articles, sacred places and ritualistic behaviors are all* about. They are labeled as sacred so they are not seen as idols of faith. Yet, they are substitutes apart from knowing directly.

[86]Not only will you be judged as falling short according to your own standard, but you will make the *illusion of hypocrisy* a real life concept.

world [87] as a battle you started in your mind. You may not know it but it is you and you alone who set you up! Remember, denial always precedes projection.

You will first have to forgive how you perceive what you perceive until you can see clearly and consistently that it is you who set you up. Time collapses whenever effect is brought to the place of cause. That place is not to be found in the world of space and time. It is in the mind that thought it.

Karma and Progression

Karma needs time and space to work itself out
Time and space need karma to justify its existence
When you find that your solution is in the mind
that made karma real
Time and space become irrelevant

Karma comes to life in the instant you make a misinterpretation real to you. The practice of defending a misinterpretation from the truth guarantees karma's continuity. As far as linear progression goes, this misinterpretation personalized as a hurtful feeling and held onto over time as resentment and guilt, skews your interactions throughout your socialized history. As you react to your interpretations of present tense situations through unconscious memories of your past, you make and collect karma. In other words, you plan a destiny based on your interpretations of a past that only exists in your memory. If it seems that you are working through one problem after another to either make someone

---

[87]In terms of large scale conflict, egos of agreed upon sacred beliefs form alliances to battle against other egos who have formed alliances out of agreed sacred beliefs. Minds can never join except in peace. This is beyond belief.

pay for their "sin" against you or for you to forgive your "sin" against another, you are either adding to or paying off a debt.

Because you do not know how to experience the present tense you will think in terms of "I should have" or "I should not have" or "you should have" or "you should not have."[88] Time is what you make when you are not interacting out of a present tense experience.

The Undoing of Karma

Every present conflict has a reason. And every reason makes the conflict irrelevant. If you do not project it away, the reason will stand clear. *The reason for your conflict is to teach you that you saw it wrong.* What else could it be?

Your misuse of mind causes you to wander through the non-events of time. Your unresolved karmic issues are right under your nose in the forms of daily happenings. The lessons you need to learn are given to you daily through the non-events you interpret and experience as conflict. What seems unresolved from the past is simply your conflict in different forms re-emerging in the present.[89] You do not experience memories. You experience the thought about that memory. Therefore, when you change your thoughts about a memory, you can have resolution now. It is this you can undo!

To heal today's conflict is the way to undo the collection of yesterday's forgotten memories. This makes the idea of working out your karma through the past, irrelevant.

---

[88]These words symbolize your *attraction to guilt.* Blame is always a projection away from recognizing your attraction to guilt.

[89]Complexity of form does not imply complexity of content. All of your seemingly different problems have the same theme in common and therefore the same solution.

Every ghost of days gone by
Will haunt the imagination of days to come
Until every problem of days gone by finds its answer now

Radical Forgiveness

Teacher of freedom, it is *radical forgiveness* that answers every problem. Forgiveness does not "bite the bullet" for what someone has done to you or for what you think you have done. That is not forgiveness. Radical forgiveness reminds you that *your unresolved conflicts of what you thought happened to you were missed opportunities to see your conflicts differently.* They remain unresolved as long as you are not ready to see them as opportunities. *Now* is the opportunity to cancel karma. There is no need to work out the past when you continue to make it right under your nose . . . in the present. Where else would you start?

Confusion teaches guilt, anger and fear. These emotions bind you to a point of view that says someone needs to be punished. There is no absolution from this point of view because this view involves loss. Karma dictates that;

As long as you believe someone should pay
You will lose

This is your destiny . . . the one you made for you to undo.

Summary

Because no thought leaves the mind that made it, your propensity to judge is hazardous to peace of mind. *Analyzing the motives of others is always risky business.* It is you through the thoughts you choose to entertain, whom you enslave or free.

Teachers of freedom, every conflict has its opportunity for resolution *now.* Forgiveness properly understood is the opportunity to see the real cause of your conflict. You are the source of what you choose to believe. And what you choose you will experience.

Any belief is a symbol of power to either bind you to that view or free you from it. When you believe your misperceptions to be the truth, that symbol of power becomes your master. It will demand from you what you believe. You will not escape the injustice you perceive until you understand that you gave it to yourself. When you understand this, you free your mind to perceive it another way. This does not suggest intellectualizing anything away. That is only wishful denial. To look again with an open mind at a decision you held fast to, is the first step to undo what you have reacted to as personally and meaningfully hurtful.

Your miracle is the opportunity to see once again what you have been reacting to was simply a mistake in perception. With misperception corrected, guilt, resentment and fear have no reason to be. Rather than remake the same mistake over and over again, now you are free to create!

Where is Karma?

Where is karma, where is its sting?
In the light of forgiveness, the bumble bee sings

When a thought that can chain
Gives way to freedom's reign
Then it is used to heal
Instead of steal

So where is karma, where is its place?
Like a falling star, it burns through space

The Lash of the Dragon's Tail

"Oh baby but the god that you been praying to
Is gonna' give you back what you been wishing
on someone else"

New Pony
Bob Dylan

Introduction

Nothing in the world of people, places and things has meaning of itself. The only meaning it has is the meaning each separate mind gives it. Everyone's perception about the world as being an individual experience, different from another, witnesses to the fact that the meaning the world has is the meaning each individual mind gives it. There are lots of different kinds of dragons running around the world that suggest;

Truth is not to be found in the world
of people, places and things

The Frustrated Learner

You may believe that you observe, perceive, evaluate and judge accurately on a consistent basis. But the fact is you perceive and project constantly based solely on what you believe about yourself. Erroneously, it is taught that we are a combination of what the world tells us we are and what we perceive ourselves to be. However, what the world seems to tell you still depends on your interpretation of it. There is no escaping the fact that;

Not only do you interpret what you encounter
You encounter what you desire to see
It is always your interpretation that you desire to see

If you are wrong about what you are, what you perceive you cannot understand. If you are deceived about what you see, you must be deceived about what you think you are! Are you projecting the error you are not, as a world that isn't, to be a witness to reinforce what you can never be? No wonder you are a frustrated student. You are trying to learn an impossible lesson.

All misperceptions come from a false sense of a self you are not. Why else would you misperceive on a daily basis? You will fear your encounter with the dragon you unknowingly made out of the self you believe to be.

"We see the world wrong and then say it deceives us"

Tagore

You may want to say that your interpretations were influenced by what happened to you; however that is your interpretation. If your interpretation of your self is mistaken, error in what you seem to perceive will result. The dragon seems real!

The "little self"

You constantly misperceive, selectively perceive, assume, judge, react to, have feelings of guilt, anger and fear[90] that you project on a world of movement and noise. But you were not born here just to die. You made the world so you could project away what you do not want to see on the inside . . . and then you seem to die.

Projection makes perception means that what you are looking at is your inner thoughts projected as an outside

---

[90] Albert Ellis; Rational Emotive Therapy.

world. Your mind is so powerful that you made a world to hide from the one thought you fear the most; *the belief that you could oppose the will of Source and succeed.* The guilt you feel from this assumed separation[91] needs an absolution that will free you from the punishment that guilt demands. But you could not look inward to Source where your solution would be found because you fear the thought that you accomplished the impossible; separation.

To avoid the punishment guilt demands, you made a world of symbols empowered by projecting your guilt upon it as a way to get rid of it.[92] Because *no thought leaves its source* you find no relief from the anger, depression and anxiety that your guilt generates. So you search the same world you made out of guilt, to hide your guilt in, for a solution / savior from the guilt you made. Through all the icons of technology, philosophy, theology, psychology, sociology, economics, history, etc., you search for a solution in a place where it cannot be found.[93]

You will not find escape from your problems in the world
The world was made so you could not escape [94]

All these substitutions are idols that you believe in someway will complete the little self you made. Because you made a little self out of guilt, it is vulnerable to pleasure, pain and death. How can you begin to understand what you perceive if you do not become conscious of your dilemma? "But the

---

[91]The root of all separation anxiety, abandonment and self esteem issues.
[92]The birth of blame.
[93]The making of karma.
[94]*The Way Home; p71*

dragon is real!" you protest, "I have been hit by its tail." So you continue to believe that what you perceive is a truth to either embrace or reject.

> *You make the victim, you make the hero*
> *You make a road to heaven or hell*
> *You wait on the crossroad of indecision*
> *Lost in the confusion of your own spell*

Attack Made Real

If reality is experienced as the expression of One Mind
There is only One Mind [95]

If there is only One Mind
Then all those individual minds you seem to see
Are you . . . an aspect [96] *of One Mind*

This is purely intellectual in concept
Until you experience it as One
Because, reality is experienced as One Mind

Because all meaning originates from One Mind, any mind that sees itself as individual does not know itself as the experience of One Mind. The experience of One Mind is the experience of knowing . . . prior to thought. To not know is to think and therefore doubt. To doubt is the vulnerability to experience fear.

---

[95]The ego resists the experience of One Mind in the name of an "individual" experience which is the kingdom of its existence. It will protest in the name of many tricky and smart arguments on its behalf to deceive you. However, "God Is" is a statement of non-duality without opposition.
[96]In the dream, the body's eyes may continue to see differences. But it is the healed mind that does not acknowledge them.

To believe that attack is real and could be accomplished is a witness that you do not know what you are, for One Mind could never attack itself. All your judgments are projections you hold against yourself. You see a flaw in another only because you do not want to see it in the self you made. This denial witnesses to the fact that the self you made is flawed and therefore vulnerable to attack. However, the self you made as a substitute against the Self you are, is the one who has made attack seem real because it believes it has accomplished the impossible; separation from Source.

Because no thought leaves its source, the self you made projects the separation as the experience of attack coming from outside. In defense of your vulnerability against the awareness of what you have projected away, you justify attack as real and defense necessary. Seemingly from the outside, you experience the backlash of the dragon's tail . . . and it's all happening in your mind.

The Meeting of Confused Minds

All symbols (forms) are neutral in meaning. Your belief that movement and noise have meaning apart from the meaning you give them, is denial of true cause and effect. Because of this belief, you do not realize that the only tension you feel comes from the meaning you give anything. In other words, you make the dragon you fear.

That you may encounter a charged reaction from another is undeniable. That you view it as negative is your interpretation. You may justify your interpretation that any particular behavior is defensive or aggressive. However, a charged encounter does not witness to a negative external influence as much as it witnesses to a clash of arbitrary beliefs between mutually confused minds.

Not only are the two of you involved in *interpreting your*

own perceptions of neutral forms for meaning, but you are both involved in an ever-changing context of social meanings that you use to defend your perceptions[97] . . . *when you lack awareness of what you really are.* So you both react fearfully to your own interpretation of the other's behaviors.

> *Attack is the defense of a justified interpretation*
> *In other words, "The way I see it is the right way!"*

Your choices in the ephemeral are always locked into dualistic selections between good or bad, right or wrong. Any choice in which someone has to lose for another to gain indicates a belief in duality. It implies that God takes sides. So you pray to a god to slay the dragon you made to defend against Truth. Radical forgiveness is the only choice possible because only radical forgiveness corrects duality.

Summary

You are either Truth or illusion, and Truth needs no defense.[98] Your judgment is merely a projection to distance you from a discomfort of what you fear you will find if you take a look at the self you think you know. Your projection masks the fact that what you seem to experience as a cause external to you is actually coming from you. The dragon you fear is the dragon you made.

> *Covering your tracks is projection's denial*
> *You can't see where it's coming from*
> *Even though it's coming from you!*

---

[97]Society is a collective hunch of symbolic meanings. You are not a product of your social context; you are a product of the guilt you refuse to forgive played out through the forms of your particular social context. It is truly amazing that an exchange of meaning occurs.

[98]*The Way Home; p28*

Teacher, do not teach the error of "psychic self defense," for it is the Truth you defend against. The discomfort you think you experience as coming from someone else[99] is what you have first done to yourself. Use your discomfort as an opportunity to look within so you can begin to approach radical forgiveness. Teacher of peace, what you project you can change. But first;

1. Be aware of what you project.

2. Then you can teach without exception that all so-called negative actions, vibes, energy, gut feelings, first impressions, etc., are merely interpretations of your own projection.[100]

3. This will bring your client's conflict within the realm of self-resolution because it comes from the mind that made it seem real.

4. This also allows them to see no basis for the idea of attack as meaningfully defendable.

See this without exception and you will free your mind to once again create. To create is to *respond to* rather than *react against.*

The beliefs you hold dear take an enormous amount of energy to defend. Your defenses witness to the fact that your beliefs are vulnerable to attack. When you no longer need to defend your beliefs, your mind is free to create. You are free to join in, to dance with, to look beyond, to rise above whatever life seems to present. What seems to happen doesn't

---

[99]This is what makes any unsuspecting form your teacher.
[100]How many times do you have to be wrong about this until you realize this is true?

matter because it has nothing to do with what You truly are. You are no longer part of the problem but part of the solution.

Through radical forgiveness you find that place where attack is not real. Here, you realize you made the dragon you fear. *You do not have to slay any dragon.* Rather, discover that if your mind is powerful enough to make a dragon to believe in, your mind is powerful enough to undo it.

Life's Continuity

"All the truth in the world adds up to one big lie"

Things Have Changed
Bob Dylan

Clarifying the Relationship Between Reincarnation, Karma & Recollection

Any Body Will Do

Clarifying the Relationship Between Reincarnation, Karma & Recollection

The world is not left by death, but by Truth

Introduction

Despite religious teaching which encourages belief in the unchanging, most people invest fearfully in the period between birth and death as if this is all there is. However, the co-existence of the changing and the unchanging is impossible. The belief that it is possible will keep you locked into the experience of dualistic thinking.[101] Because the co-existence of change and the eternal is impossible, to experience change is to deny the eternal.

Once you have invested in dualistic thinking and thus the experience of ever-changing time, one cycle or a million cycles is just as meaningless. Therefore, whether or not reincarnation, karma and recollection are real, is not the issue. The question for those who believe in reincarnation, karma and recollection is; are they helpful in your spiritual progress[102] towards your awakening from these concepts altogether? Through this perspective do the concepts of reincarnation, karma and recollection have value.

Only one reality is possible and it is experienced as "known." This is beyond any thought of duality experienced through the senses. Those who identify with the temporal will witness the duality of change and experience the memory of time in the present moment, as if it is real.

---

[101]Experience through thinking and comparing, e.g. good and bad, right and wrong, up and down, hot and cold, life and death, etc.
[102]This does not imply an evolution of the soul.

Insanity's Choice

To face this predicament honestly, one must admit that nothing of the body can be kept beyond the death of the body. Insanity however, dictates that it is practical and prudent for one to identify with, invest in and accumulate securities for the life experience of the body. This attempt to invest in the fleeting, results in the making of time and space[103] by the mind that looks for clarification and meaning through the body's eyes. This misplaced identity is the reason that change, growth, healing and death become fearful concepts

Your primary distraction to hearing the call home is the idea that the self is a body, subject to the temporal and therefore to death. If you were to generalize this lesson too every area of your life, you would recognize the insanity of your choices to invest in what the body's eyes perceive as security. You have been vigilant to invest in and defend the means for conflict. To look at this can be fearful indeed. Until you do, the self is but a wanderer weaving its way through the conflict it perceives. Unknowingly, in your attempt to find a home in the fleeting, change has been made by you as a witness to the inevitability of death. In truth, the cycles of change witness to neither life nor death.[104] For in the end;

Change, which you are not
Provides no meaning for what you are

Reincarnation is but a dream of going into a body again . . . the cycle of change.

---

[103]Time and space are conditions needed for the fleeting to exist just as the fleeting justifies the experience of time and space.
[104]*The Way Home; p173-176*

What Recollection Is

In the whirlwinds of reincarnation and karma, life seems to be separate and discontinuous. Each birth and death constitutes the measurement of one's so-called life experience in a body.[105] Reincarnation and karma do not address what happens between these body-lives. In fact, the interludes[106] seem not to be a form of life at all. The definition of life is inextricably tied to the body experience.

Recollection is a present thought experience of a past body life,[107] remembered by a mind relaxed of self-imposed limits. With these limits suspended, your mind has the potential to remember memories of people, places and events of a past body experience . . . in the present moment. It is as simple as imagining each day of your life to symbolize a body life you once had. It is like remembering what you did yesterday in today's present moment. The only difference is that you are remembering a yesterday of a past body experience.

---

[105]The examination of all these collected birth and death cycles involves a regression into one's past body experiences. Regression is the experience of recollection's skip through time; the illusion of looking back. Thus does one's past life regression *seem to be* the study of one's karmic cycle through time gone by . . . in the moment that is always present.

[106]These interludes (after body death and before body birth) are experiences free of the limits of body wants, needs and desires. This is not heaven because you still don't remember "God Is." It is the other side of the karmic loop of your dream of reincarnation. When your projected guilt catches up with you, you reincarnate. Death is not the way out, waking up is.

[107]The use of the term "past life" is a misnomer. You don't really die to live again. "Past body experience" is a more accurate term. You have experienced the illusion of many bodies, but always in the present moment. You only have one life . . . and that life you experience as One . . . in the eternal now.

Reincarnation is a dream of going into a body again. *Karma* is the destiny you act out dependent upon how you interpret and thus experience the symbols of that dream. *Recollection* is remembering the experience of a part of the dream. Like reincarnation and karma, recollection derives its influence from identification with the temporal order of things. However, unlike reincarnation and karma, recollection freely skips through time as an opportunity to collapse time all together. The collapse of time seems to be a process that undoes reincarnation and karma.

Recollection's Usefulness

An unresolved past,[108] plans for future possibilities
This blocks your awareness of
your present experience in Source

You have misused your memory for so long that you do not understand that it can be used as an opportunity for you to remember your "present" experience in Source. Recollection is useful in showing that the self-imposed limitations of body-birth and body-death are not real to the mind that can skip through the memories of time. Once these limits are recognized as impermanent, your present body experience cannot be taken seriously. Said another way, recollection, like astral mobility, reminds you that you have been locked into the belief of an ephemeral experience.[109]

---

[108]This in the end means *any memory* because your experience in Source is a timeless presence. Even a fond memory has nothing to do with knowing Being.

[109]You are not having an ephemeral experience because you are in a body. You seem to be having an ephemeral experience because *you believe* you are a body.

The ephemeral is a limiting experience that has nothing to do with what you are. To recall the memory of a past body experience in a seemingly present body gives your mind a powerful learning opportunity to rethink everything you think your body is. It can help you take another look at what you have mistaken as true. Recollection aids in the healing of your mind by reminding it of the self-imposed limits it has accepted to unknowingly imprison itself.

The Part Forgiveness Plays

You believe you accomplished the impossible; that you have severed your relationship from Source and buried the memory of it in times past. You made the body to hide from this guilt not knowing that your body was made out of guilt as the ultimate symbol of your separation from Source. Because the world was made so you could not escape your dilemma, you deal with guilt by either projecting it away as anger and blame or accepting your just punishment through shame and pain. In the world of ever-changing forms, these seem to be your choices. But they are both illusion. *The real choice is to forgive your experiences of what you took as real but never was. All of them!*

Forgiveness is like the process of editing a movie. A director needs to edit pieces out that are irrelevant to the story. By reviewing what does and doesn't work, he finds things to edit out onto the cutting floor. In the movies, the editing process culminates in a cohesive story. By removing what distracted from the whole, the director is able to present the story he envisioned. If you compare your life to a movie, your "editing" process is accomplished through forgiveness. With its application to every aspect of your story, you gradually edit out the irrelevant. Your speed-up is the shortening of the movie called your life. Eventually, through forgiveness you come to realize that you do not have a story to tell because it has all been edited to the cutting floor. In the end the last illusion is forgiveness.

Blocks to Remembering Removed

With no story to invest in, you wake up to a reality other than the movie you thought was real. When your dream is on the cutting floor after finishing the work of all your forgiveness lessons, your ego is gone. There is nothing that interferes with your experience of the truth of what you are. Your need to reincarnate out of guilt to undo guilt is no longer necessary because . . . you no longer have any guilt to undo. You remember the experience of what you really are. Your work of forgiveness undoes the karma that seemed to give you a past to undo in the future. The karmic destiny you made for yourself is undone. With karma gone, there is no past to recall and forgive.

You may seem to be moving forward but actually you have an illusion of moving back through the collected memories of your mind. You are moving to undo the first and only error that you buried under all the memories of your mind; the belief you can oppose the will of Source and succeed. Any recollected memory of a past body experience, properly interpreted as an opportunity to free your mind of self-imposed limits of belief, becomes a speed-up to stir you to remember what you vaguely recall; the experience of One Mind.

The View from Your Center

Reincarnation is like a hurricane. In the center is peaceful calm. For a brief instant you look out. The dazzling and ever-changing whirlwind of mystification catches the eye of the mind. Disorientation follows and with your back to the calm, you walk into a storm. Disorientation leads to fear as you panic about being lost. Not able to remember your way back you identify with a body to be your home of safety. Not realizing that your alliance with a body-self idea to find safety from fear actually intensifies your fear, you become preoccupied with finding a place to rest so you can hold fear at bay. Forgetting your place of calm, you build your little kingdom of distractions[110] as an attempt to convince yourself that this new body will be your home of safety. You have been trying to convince yourself of this over many body life experiences. However, all your icons are nothing but substitutions that reflect your discontent with what you have settled for. Those in the center see all, know all, and are all.

Choose your center, and choose it well
One choice extends peace
The other breeds hell

Coming home is your mind's process of stepping out of the whirlwind of reincarnation. This process is a focused journey to remember your center of calm. As you move towards your center, the fog lessons. As the fog decreases you see more clearly opportunities for joy. It was hard to see these opportunities in the whirlwind of time. In fact, you often saw them as hardships. But now, these opportunities are frequent. Like manna from heaven,[111] they feed your focus for nothing but the remembrance of One Mind. Within your center of calm, no hurricane exists. *Mind's ability to rethink everything, is mind's ability to choose again a center other than the limiting time frame one calls a body. This is your journey towards the memory of your creations!*

In the center is Source. Those who no longer identify with

---

[110]The ever-changing is but one big substitution of distractions.
[111]Exodus 16; John 6:31-33. *The Way Home; p 68*

a body *image* as "self" have no investment in that which returns to dust. They wake up. However, the shedding of a
body is not death but the continuity of your dream of life . . .
in another fashion. Let me clarify; to shed a body *image* is to
wake up. To shed the body is but a change from one dream
to another to another until you shed your investment in a
body *image* all together. The world is not left by death. It is
left by waking up.

What is life?
It is the flash of a butterfly in the night
It is the little shadow which runs across the grass
And loses itself in the sunset
There is no death
Only a change of worlds

Crowfoot Chief Seattle

Reincarnation and karma reflect an investment in the fleeting. They are explanations of your projection through a world
of change. Because change is your investment in what you
are not, you seem to die again and again and again until you
remember the "Eternal I Am." Recollection is a tool you can
use when it reminds you of the changeless You.

Life's Continuity

The world is not left by death, but by truth

Teacher, your experience of the ever-changing suggests
that the death of a body is the end of that life. Yet, logic
dictates that within the illusion of a past that is not, and a
future that will never be, is an ever present birthing process

from life to life. "Now" you are, though you seem to be a body. If you have always been "now," then it is only the external forms that have changed along with the body you seem to be. Therefore, changing scenarios of one body as well as many bodies experienced in the "now" cannot be taken seriously as meaningfully real.

Whether it is one body life or a million body lives, the undoing of reincarnation becomes the simple lesson of realizing that you are not the body you seem to inhabit.[112] The idea of reincarnation exists because of your belief in a body-self image. Raising the validity of this image to doubt is to look towards something more expansive in experience and changeless in the "now."

Any Present Moment Will Do

Any moment you relax the limitations your mind puts on the body is an opportunity to experience a memory of a past body experience. This is not time travel. It is only a memory held in the mind. Because you are the mind of Source, there is nowhere else . . . except in a dream that seems to be.

When you were living in yesterday, what tense were you in? The present. When tomorrow arrives, what tense will you be in? The present. When are you *not* living in the present?[113] Never. Because recollecting is the experience of a memory in any present moment, it witnesses to the fact that time does not exist but in the mind that thinks it.

No matter what form your presenting problem seems to

---

[112]Progress measured as external change is the illusion of evolution. Gaining awareness regarding how your mind works is the process of waking up to the truth of what you already are.

[113]Though you do not always experience it, you always live in the present. Because your mind is out of control you allow it to wander into experiencing tenses that are not real. This is the experience of illusion. You scarcely remember the experience of this moment.

be, reincarnation is but the dream of experiencing this problem over and over again (karma). Memory makes a past seem real, gone and therefore untouchable to change. However, because your present conflict is a symbol of an ancient hate, it is through forgiving your *current* perception[114] of it that undoes time and therefore reincarnation. Through forgiving your presenting problem, you undo a part of your collective memory that collapses time, bringing you closer to your awakening.

Summary

Each event in your present body experience is an opportunity to collapse time; to be born anew by undoing karma. Any moment you choose release from the investment of an ephemeral experience is also an instant of rebirth.[115]

Your beliefs in the ever-changing are substitutes that hide what you are. Until you unlearn the lessons that the birth to death cycle provides, you will prepare again to die to the birthing process of reincarnation. Forgiving your perceptions of what you thought about the ever-changing, releases you from this karmic cycle.

There'll come a time when most of us return here
Brought back by our desire to be, a perfect entity
Living through a million years of crying
Until you've realized the Art of Dying

Art of Dying
George Harrison

---

[114]It is not about what happened that lives on; it is a memory of how you perceived it that lives on and is brought to your awareness by a present conflict.

[115]A collapse of time is an arousing from a slumber experienced as an epiphany, a mystical experience, an expansion of awareness.

Any Body Will Do

You may come back to fulfill a contract [116]
But if the ephemeral is the condition you come back to
Then the conditions you come back to, belong to chance

Introduction

You may be one who allows for the idea of reincarnation; the dream of returning to an ephemeral body to learn a lesson, to undo karma. But do not allow for the thought that you enter a particular body for a particular life style to learn a particular lesson. This error suggests that your scenarios are *particularly important* in order to learn the lesson you are "meant to learn." Instead, realize the ephemeral is all the same as far as illusion goes. It is not the situation you find yourself in that decides your fate. Rather, it is your interpretation of any situation that decides your journey through the illusion. In other words;

It's not what happens that matters
It's how you think about what happens that matters
And this you can change!

Comparing One Illusion to Another

Because the world that seems to be outside of your mind is not separate from your thoughts, there are *no limits* to how you may choose to perceive it. Nor is the particular body type you project relevant. If the only meaningful function in time is to forgive your interpretations, there is no real relevance to red, yellow, white, or black. Being male versus female makes no difference. Being challenged or competent in any form

---

[116]Every unforgiving thought is a contract to undo karma.

does not impact the lessons of forgiveness. Your religious, political, cultural or economic conditions are irrelevant to what you must learn. No matter what you appear to be or the situations you find yourself in, forgiveness levels the playing field because it teaches that your opportunity for miracles is any where, at any time, in any body form.

Worshiping at the Altar of "Social Conditioning"

Simply stated, you are born because of unconscious guilt. You play this guilt out through the environment you find yourself in. So called social conditioning is a way to play your guilt out. To try and explain why you are the way you are because of social conditioning has enormous problems with massive contradictions. To try and make social conditioning a cause of attitude and behavior is an attempt to make the world real.

John Locke[117] once postulated "Tabula Rasa"[118] which is the theory that at birth the mind is completely empty and unencumbered by innate desire, drives, etc. Consequently, all knowledge is based upon experience. In essence, he believed that we are all born with a blank slate. What you become depends on how your parents and society at large raise you. B F Skinner[119] and other behaviorists took it a step further, stating that if we can make a lion jump through a hoop of fire, if we can make an elephant dance on two legs,

---

[117]English philosopher and political theorist (1632-1704); began the empiricist tradition that believes all knowledge is derived through the experiences of the senses rather than being innate.

[118]Latin for "blank slate."

[119]American psychologist (1904-1990); developed the theory of operant conditioning; the idea that behavior is determined by its consequences, be they reinforcements or punishments. Skinner believed that the only scientific approach to psychology was one that studied behaviors, not internal mental processes.

if we can make dolphins jump through hoops in the air, if we can make chimpanzees communicate through symbols, then we can turn your child into anything we want through a conditioning of consistent, successive approximations (rewarding desirable behavior after the fact), aversive stimuli (punishing undesirable behaviors), and negative reinforcement (ignoring the behavior).

However, if you think about when your child was born, even before you had an opportunity to nurture and train them, there was something unique about them from the beginning. Maybe under the guise of a needy or content infant there was a personality,[120] all its own. Working with the presentation of this personality, as the child grew you would attempt to reinforce desirable behaviors and attitudes and attempt to extinguish undesirable behaviors and attitudes. Sometimes, some of the things you did to modify your child's behaviors seemed to work. Sometimes, nothing you did worked. Sometimes behaviors and attitudes would come and go all on their own.

Did you come to this life "innocent" to be conditioned out of it? When did you teach your child the behaviors of the "terrible twos?" Maybe they brought it with them? Why does one child exhibit that kind of behavior when another child of the same family does not? When did you teach your child to be impulsive about decision making? Maybe they brought it with them? Where did your child's attitude to act out come from? They brought it with them? When did you teach your child to be self destructive with alcohol and drugs?[121] Maybe they brought it with them? You may say that you modeled bad

---

[120]The illusion of traits, qualities, characteristics, short comings, etc.
[121]*Healing the Wound: The Family's Journey through Chemical Dependency; p14-20*

behavior. How come they didn't all learn it? You may say that one child saw your behavior and decided to do it differently. Maybe they brought that choice with them?

Though the contradictions to how you raised your child and how they turned out are enormous, you selectively find witnesses to justify guilt and blame as explanations for behaviors that have no consistent explanation for how your children turned out. Who taught you to resist this message? Maybe you brought resistance with you? After all these years of education and wisdom writing, how come there is no definitive book on child raising? Maybe, no matter what you do, there is an individuality about them that is a done deal at birth.

If you understand, things are the way they are
If you do not understand, things are the way they are

Zen proverb

No matter how you think about it and fearfully try to protect your children from self-destruction, just like yourself, they have their own journey; a lesson to learn that belongs to that individual alone. In the light of this you can practice radical forgiveness. You can forgive yourself for the responsibility you thought was yours because in the bigger picture it belongs to the destiny of their karma.

Being a parent may seem to give you certain social responsibilities but that does not make you responsible for a child's destiny. This is not an excuse for how you parent or a justification to abdicate parental involvement, but it does give you another view as to "what happened?"

Nature vs. Nurture
The "nature" theory of personality development doesn't

explain why your child turns out the way they do. Yes, it is true that you can attribute color of eyes, hair, complexion, family mannerisms and mental illnesses, etc., to genetic influence or inheritance. However, within each family you find totally different personalities and perceptions on how to interpret life situations being acted out through genetic predispositions.

If you look closely, these personality differences are independent of nature and nurture. Remember, your children at birth had something about them that was already there. Just like yourself, all through your child's growing up, no matter what you did to redirect them, they did what they thought. Within the limits of their genetic blue print you may have been involved in behavior modification. However it was up to each of us to choose our own interpretation of life events. How are you to explain this?

Beneath the controversy of nature vs. nurture is the work of karma. Karma is your story because it is the destiny you made . . . the destiny for you to undo. Within this context, the controversy of nature vs. nurture becomes irrelevant.

Forgetting What You Really Are

Because Source created you out of Itself, you remain true. The belief that you can oppose the Will of Source and succeed is an error that can only breed guilt. And guilt always fears punishment. You dream of incarnating[122] out of guilt as a way to escape from the punishment you fear. This is the agenda you bring with you at birth. Because denial precedes projection, you forget this whole process. You may argue that social conditioning prevented you from knowing who you

---

[122]Projecting a mental image is what dreaming is; you perceive what you project rather than know what you are.

are,[123] but the truth is you were born because you don't know the Self you already are. You didn't forget after the birthing process, you were 'born' because you forgot. Birth, infancy, and childhood are part of the illusion that our innocence can be taken from us.

Social conditioning is not a cause of confusion; it is an effect of already being confused. It is an effect of the original error to hide from the Truth of the matter. It is a distraction, an explanation to avoid dealing with the original error.

In the mind of Source, you are an expression of pure love. Any thought apart from that expression projects a body out of guilt, to hide guilt. Forgiveness is the only function meaningful in time because it is your journey to undo guilt. There is nothing else. One works to make the world real through investment in it, only to dream of dying again. Another works to undo guilt by seeing the world for what it really is. This is what real choice is about. Which do you choose? That is your journey, your destiny to fulfill! And any body, time or place will do.

Any Situation Will Do

The reason body types, sexual identity, genetic makeup, social class and conditioning are irrelevant is because the lesson for you to learn transcends the conditions of ever-changing forms. The world is just a backdrop; a projection out of guilt to hide your guilt. Now it is for you to use the world of events as opportunities to facilitate the lessons you need, to undo guilt. To believe that these external conditions are particularly important is to deny the simple fact;

---

[123]The making of the illusion of self-esteem issues.

Forgiving your interpretation of any situation
Makes every situation irrelevant
When you generalize this lesson to every situation

You proclaim sexual, cultural, personality differences as significantly important to defend the illusion of individuality. You even "honor" these differences as a way to make the world's troubles understandable and therefore solvable.[124] All this explaining is but a delay tactic from remembering the experience we all share as One, beyond the differences of a body.

All healing is through the experience of One Mind
Not in analyzing how you are different

The body's eyes will see differences but it is the healed mind that does not acknowledge them. Idolizing differences is what breeds anger, guilt and fear. The undoing of these irrelevant conditions through radical forgiveness is what is needed to undo fixed perceptions. Radical forgiveness is needed to shift your perception away from the illusion of a hierarchy of importance.[125]

The form of your life situation is irrelevant. The only relevance is choosing to see the lesson presented as an opportunity to heal. One person suffers in a so-called easy life of privilege. Another seems to rise above circumstances that others see as hardships. One person uses their interpretation of life to be bitter. Another sees their life as an opportunity to extend love. The question asked and answered in every situation is; what do you want to make it mean? Remember;

---

[124]Is there such a thing as a noble open-minded altruistic ego? *The Way Home; p145*
[125]This hierarchy is *always* subject to change.

It's not what happens that matters
It's how you think about what happens that matters

It is common to argue that your life situation is relevant. However, it is your perception of any life situation that decides its relevance to you. The miracle interprets every situation as an opportunity for you to see it as it always is; a meaningless effect of the mind, mistaken as something pleasurably or fearfully real.

The miracle of forgiving your perception of any given situation shows you that the situation was never the relevant factor. You finally used the situation to free your mind of its interpretation.

Summary

Teacher of healing, though it may appear so, your clients' problems are not coming from outside of them. It is the miracle that shows you another way to look at it. This is what makes you a healed healer. Now it becomes clear that the only release is through the mind that made the situation seem real. Any situation will do. Any situation that catches your attention is relevant. Only in this does it have value. Apart from that, what do you want to make it mean? When you are ready the teacher will appear . . . usually in a form least expected.

If you need to say "There is a reason for this event" then say it and know that it is not about the event anymore. It is the reason that makes the event meaningless. No matter how diverse your presenting problems may appear they all provide you an opportunity for one reason . . . to undo your perceived guilt through forgiving your perception of it . . . so you can wake up![126]

---

[126]*The Way Home; p137-138*

It's not what happens that matters
It's how you think about what happens that matters
And this you can change!

Your up-bringing, genetic makeup, social conditioning and life situations are not your problems, they merely reflect the cause. The cause is a mind confused about what it thinks it is. Because you made "nothing" mean something, you can change your mind about it.[127] You can let it remind you without exception that it is your opportunity to remember your innocence . . . an innocence that remains safe beyond the nothingness you desired. Choose again.

---

[127] *The Way Home; p146*

Section II

Symbols of Power
and
Your Creative Self

Your experience of One Mind
Is the expression of your creative self
Everything else is your brush on canvas

Your Creative Self

When fear is gone your creations shine

Healing as an Expression of Your Creative Self

Self Deception: The Primary Block to Expressing Your Creative Self

Communicating from Your Creative Self

Healing as an Expression of Your Creative Self

You will know your creations on this side of the veil
They will remind you that your innocence
is already accomplished

Introduction

As creation, your experience of reality is shared.[128] However, you seem to experience the illusion of an individual self.[129] Therefore, creating is something you have to learn, until you remember the experience of reality as One.

The Search

Minds do not know need, but bodies do. Your experience of need is justified by your identification with a body as if it is your center of being. Because of the strange situation you find yourself in, your creations[130] are translated as extensions through your body until you remember your creations through the remembrance of One Mind.

You use your hand to move the brush, but it is the mind that paints the picture. You use your wealth to provide for another, but it is the mind that perceives the need. A mind cluttered, undecided, and distracted by the needs of a body has to work hard at creating. It longs for the experience of release from the limits it has placed upon itself.

Your yearning for release takes many forms. You go to war in the name of freedom and peace. You fight to defend sacred icons in the name of truth. You defend territory you think is

---

[128]Not shared as if by everyone but rather experienced as One.
[129]The experience of a separate reality is a self-validating delusion that denies you the remembrance of the experience of One Mind.
[130]Abilities, gifts, talents, etc.

yours to possess. In the name of "achievement" you become addicted to work, alcohol, drugs, food, money, relationships, things, etc., looking for that experience of release. You ingratiate the body with flashy ornaments as attractions to who you want to be. Yet, happiness eludes you. "Somewhere out there it is to be found" you say. You find temporary relief, but you never find that experience of release you search for. Because the body's eyes perceive duality, polarity and opposition in everything it looks upon, your mind experiences the conflict of divided goals. How can a mind create as it wanders through the non-events of time when it is cluttered, undecided, divided and distracted?

Because you are the expression of freedom through Source, to limit is to make sick. Your mind is sick, not your body because you have limited your Eternal Creations to be forms. Any symbol is an idol when it is used to limit your expression of creation. It is a limit when you believe it can bring you the happiness / security you desire. Yet, what you experience is a temporary relief, a momentary pleasure, to search again and again for another idol to satisfy. Decide for any form of limitation in search of happiness and you will receive the experience of lack.

Your Primary Need

Because you are not the needs and limits of the body, your creations constantly flow within you looking for expression. You do not recognize this because of a preoccupation with a body that is actually outside of you. Your experience of distractions and needs is not good or bad, right or wrong. They merely witness to the limits you have given yourself. They are substitutions that block your awareness of your creative spirit. This blocked awareness is projected as beliefs; judgments of anger, guilt and fear. That is why *the body you seem to be needs to be placed into proper perspective.* You will project these limits on your world canvas you have mistaken for real. Anger, guilt and fear are always perceived as justified even though they are the results of a limiting view through selective judgments. Again, projection always precedes perception. Though you do not knowingly ask for limitation, what you wish for you always find . . . not always in the form you desired.

If you perceive your self as lacking, you will seek for completion. This insanity is your search for completion in a world that demonstrates lack.[131] Trying to achieve an impossible goal is the definition of a frustrated learner. However, this expression of your desire to heal can be translated through your creative spirit.

Willingness to listen is your primary need. It goes along with the recognition that *you do not know as you think.*[132] This is your first step towards remembering your creations. Your ability to exercise discipline of mind depends on your willingness to listen to your internal guide. It is your voice for peace of mind. Your primary block to listening is the belief that what you think you see and hear you think you understand! Understand this; the body's eyes perceive conflict. Understand that beliefs that limit your experience of One Mind are your symbols of sickness.

> *To see your client as sick*
> *is your symbol of sickness, not theirs!*

In whatever form your creative self chooses for expression, you will be reminding your clients to identify, clarify, express

---

[131]It's all happening in your mind. There is no "out there."
[132]The Dao Te Ching; #71

and look beyond the symbols of sickness they present . . . *so you can heal.* Listen to them.

Your willingness to accept the truth
of what your client represents
Becomes your door to being a healed healer

You cannot be available to create until you look at what your client truly represents. What they are is what your mind tells them they are, and that is what you first think of you! Your client either symbolizes your innocence of One Mind or the sickness of your individual self. You choose how to perceive your projection. One perception is like a wall, one is like a door. Both views stand symbolically between your inner self and the expression of your creations. One way of seeing keeps you trapped, the other sets you free.

Learning to be available to your inner self opens you to experience and express the flow of your creations. The more you are able to slip beyond beliefs into the flow of freedom, the more you will be able to use the troubles and distractions of your life as inspirations through which you express your creations. Again, understand; your mind is cluttered, distracted and deceived in what it thinks it sees. It always manifests what it first desired. This is the power your mind has to either create abundance[133] or experience the projection of confusion and loss.

Did the world deceive you?
Or are you using the world
to deceive yourself?

---

[133]Abundance is not the collection of idols for happiness. It is experiencing what you are in Truth. *The Way Home; p152-154*

Being Emptied

Are the substitutions you use to free you, blocks to express-ing your creative process?

> *Before a vessel can be filled with new wine*
> *The old must be drained*

> *Going through a process?*
> *Take heart, disorientation beckons*

> *None of your old ideas work?*
> *Be glad, you're just being emptied*

Your release to extend and create involves your willingness to place the body you seem to inhabit into proper perspec-tive. The experience of a free mind naturally expresses its own creations. Engage your passion but don't desire to possess or control outcomes.

> *It is not my body that demands death*
> *It is my demands on the body that dictate death*
> *Today I release my body from the demands I put on it*
> *So it can serve a purpose for my healing*

Trying to control outcomes is a perceived lack that breeds anxiety, depression and anger. However, no matter what you do, think or say, you are playing a part in the bigger picture. There is a way to participate in the illusion without investing in what your part means.

> *The whole is greater than the sum of its parts*
> *Your part is to be available to the whole*

Healer, it is necessary to release the tendency to want to control therapeutic outcomes. To create is to allow the present moment to be what it is without an idea of what the outcome should be. In this way you participate as part of what you create. If your creation is inspired through the brush stroke of love, you will attract the colors of healing, peace and unity. If you bring cloaked coercion into the process, you will produce confusion, strife and division.

The Miracle of Healing

A mind unaware of its own decision to limit itself is limited in its ability to create. When you perceive another as wrong, you are focused on the level of dualistic thinking which breeds interpretations of conflict. Your alternatives to perceive are limited to the level of outward appearances. Contrary to what you may think, *to perceive another as wrong reveals a conflict within you.* This is unknown to you because you want to see your thoughts of conflict projected outside of you, in another. Because you see your thoughts projected on a form outside of your individual mind, you justify that what you see must be true because you see it there!

> *"You believe in what you made*
> *because it was made by your belief in it"* [134]

Self righteous anger is the refusal to see that what you see is your own reflection. All you are witnessing to is your thoughts, projected on some unsuspecting passerby. Alone as a separate body, you seek the ego alliances of other separate bodies. This is your sickness embodied by your fixed

[134]A Course in Miracles

belief, your symbol of power. No one can release you to change your mind but you alone.

Truth is not established by looking to the world

Your ability to create is not based on evaluations or judgments of something "outside." Your evaluations are expressions of what you think on the inside. Your creations are a continuous internal flow without the need of anything external. The external is merely your canvas, which reflects the internal. The external may be a stimulus that awakens creation within you, but it is still an effect or extension of mind's creation and not a cause. Changing your mind about the limits of how you will interpret and therefore experience the external, is a reflection of an inner process that allows you the opportunity to freely express your natural state as creation.

Do not set limits on
what you believe can be done through you
So you can accept what can be done for you

This is the miracle of healing.

Potential

Questions such as "what is my purpose?" and "how am I to be used?" reflect the idea of future possibilities. There is nothing wrong with this as long as it is out of the now.

So keep on playing those mind games together
Faith in the future out of the now

Mind Games
John Lennon

However, the hope of a future possibility can rob you of your opportunity to be available to create NOW! Because an open mind does not need to plan, these questions become unimportant. An open mind always sees the opportunity as it arrives NOW. Looking for tomorrow's opportunity causes you to overlook the opportunity presented NOW! An open mind trusts that it will see the blocks your mind presents as what they always were, the opportunities you were waiting for. A mind free to create will find Wisdom not of its own but through the Mind we all know as One.

When you have questions about tomorrow, it is always out of doubt. In the realm of doubt, your choices are always between two illusions.[135] That is not a real choice, and no real answer can come of it. The healing response would be to use doubt as a means to recognize there is a bigger picture than the question at hand. Looking through the immediate question is a choice waiting for you not of the world though you seem to be choosing between forms in the world. You can never have all the information you need in the world of the fleeting to feel secure. If the door you face opens, walk in.[136] Any more than this is mindless thinking.

Availability

To begin expressing your creative self, there is only one thing you need to do . . . be willing.

To create is to share . . . To share is to create
By reinterpreting the ability to attack
into the ability to share
You translate what you have made
into what you are . . . Creation!

---

[135] *The Way Home; p55-57*
[136] *The Way Home; p190*

Teacher, be willing to see the ephemeral as the nothing-ness it is and you will not perceive attack as anything per-sonal.[137] When you are free to look beyond fear, you recognize everyone mistakes the ephemeral as real and takes it personally. So do you. When you stop using all your energy to defend your interpretation of nothing, you allow your creations to manifest themselves through your joyful dance of knowing.

The development and maturation of any ability involves your willingness to rethink your beliefs about everything. Your suspension of all beliefs allows you the space to create spontaneously in ways you never imagined. Not only do you extend your inspirations through the paintbrush, you also participate as part of the brush as you allow creation to flow through you. Availability knows no boundaries. It is free be-yond any wish to limit, allowing you the opportunity to meet any need of the moment.

It is not necessary for you to conquer or change or even heal the world.[138] By simply being willing to expend the effort it takes to be available, you will be shown what to do.

The Need for Direction

You will have opportunities to study under a variety of teachers, but you do not need to limit yourself to any partic-ular person or institution for direction.[139] However, you do need direction! Because your mind lacks discipline to a greater degree than you want to believe, a daily reminder is

---

[137]Not only do you cease interpreting attack as personal, you do not inter-pret anything as attack.

[138]*The Way Home; p35*

[139]I am not against having a teacher or guru as an aid for redirection, just like this book is for redirection. But if they are not about redirecting you to look inside to find you, they are just another distraction of delay.

most helpful to speed you along your way. Meditations of all sorts are available to help teach your mind the discipline of uninterrupted focus. Allow for a curriculum that is best suited to your needs and style of learning.

The practice of application leads to experience

Whatever practice you choose, extend love as your motivation for what you do. This overcomes all fear and teaches you to hear your inner voice. Doubt may be involved in the process of learning but do not worry. Once you start, your outcome is certain. With practice, those vague gut feelings will strengthen into the knowingness of your inner voice. Repetition is essential to learning.

Summary

Stated simply, to express your creative self involves your availability to access and translate the natural flow of your creative Spirit. Your canvas may be the ever-changing but it is your Spirit within that envisions, manifests and expresses.[140] This availability starts with an attitude of meditative discipline. Learning first hand about the power of your mind through training provides you an aspect of possibility that reaches far beyond the distractions and perceived limits of the body. Because creative spirit allows rather than confines, any need to be both creative and in control of the outcome is a contradiction. Therefore;

It is not for you to evaluate
the outcome of your gift
It is for you to give them

---

[140] *The Way Home: p24-26*

Healer, teacher, metaphysician, it is the belief that you are separate from your Creator that makes you sick. *All sickness is symbolic* of that belief. Because that belief is an error, not only is healing possible, it is inevitable. You deal with the symbols your client presents because those are the symbols that represent their belief in sickness. To see their symbols as what they are, allows you the inspiration of any given moment to create and express healing beyond the limits of what any symbol represents.

The body you inhabit is not an end
Like a paintbrush, it is a means of extension . . .
Through which you paint your reflection . . .
On the canvas of space and time

Self Deception: The Primary Block to Expressing Your Creative Self

Because the guiltless mind needs no protection
Your defenses are attempts to protect the guilt you made
. . . from the Truth

Introduction

Defensiveness is nothing more than a reflection of what you do not want to see in yourself. The ego's attempt to confuse and complicate simplicity is enormous. It confuses you by telling you what your problem is and then promises to show you the way out. Because the ego is a concept and not reality, the only place it can exist is in the part of the mind that has given itself over to the illusion of a body experience.

When you advocate on behalf of the experience of an individual reality you become conflicted. When your mind is split between the experience of One Mind and the need to defend an individual reality, only fear can result.

That which was made out of fear always needs protection
Because it is not the truth

The Experience of Self Deception

You do not know you are in self-deception. That is why you are unaware of the dream you project and experience as real. This can be rationalized as semantics to those who wish to remain deceived. However, you spend your life asleep, aware of only a fraction of your thoughts. Under the surface of your awareness, like an iceberg, almost all of what you are thinking remains hidden or unconscious. Your sleep dreams tell you something is there, you just don't know how much. Because your mind is making decisions continually under the surface, you are making *back door deals* that give you thoughts and feelings you don't always understand.

While this is going on, in a world of people, places and circumstances, relationships are established through contrast and comparison. In the world of individual bodies there is truth to the statement "Beauty belongs to the eye of the beholder." So does ugliness. For example, if there is rich, there must be poor. To complicate matters, there is a whole range of wealth in between. Furthermore, you can be poor compared to one person, yet wealthy when compared to someone else. Nothing in this belief system exists without such relative relationships. Through sensing and perceiving, your identity as a body requires constant adaptation on the basis of these external associations. The senses naturally serve the body by responding to its concern for survival. Thus the idea of protection becomes a real life experience to the mind that perceives itself as a body.

Because the body exemplifies limitation, it experiences weakness in itself and seeks protection. But only a body can seem to be hurt, never your mind. Your mind only assumes these feelings out of a confusion of identity. It is only through this mistaken assumption of identity that your mind feels pain, for it is within *the power of your mind* to experience what it assumes to be true.

When you lie to yourself it is easy to believe any lie
And not know that you are lying to yourself

When you are experiencing the effects of your mind as if it is something outside of you, it is *almost* impossible to imagine that your mind made the world you see. You live pleasure and pain, hot and cold, good and bad, sickness and health as if they are caused by an outer reality.

You project the world you see
And experience it as if it is something outside your mind
Don't you know this?

A Split Mind

Your experience of reality is the experience of One Mind. The projection of a problem outside of you creates the appearance of an inner and outer world. Maintaining this split requires an enormous amount of energy. Self-deception becomes its primary means. With all the substitutions of beliefs you acquire to fill your outer world, you do not remember the experience of One Mind. Only anger, guilt, depression and fear can result. All lies are experienced and defended as truth when you choose to believe them.

If you believe what you believe will save you
The truth will scare you
Truth needs no defense. Lies do

You see your problems as "out there" only because you fear to look inward to see the deceit you have harbored within. You are not who you think you are. *All your adaptations are your attempts to establish what you are not.* Your refusal to see this deception is the dream you make. In your dream you project your conflict as problems "out there" and away from you. Perceived this way, it now seems that you can deal with your many problems using many substitutions,[141] thereby reinforcing self deceit. Your substitutions may bring some relief some of the time, they may even seem to heal . . . only to come back in a different form hidden in

---

[141]Rather than discount your outer world, psychology, philosophy, sociology and theology are attempts to understand and thus justify your outer world as real.

self-deception. This is because your problem is not out there. "Out there" was made by a split mind.

Self deceit always experiences fear. You defend yourself against truth with distractions. This is not protection; this is delay and an invitation to insanity.

Your Reflection as a Symbol of Power

To identify with is to heal. To judge is to separate. To deny your self-made condemnation is to project it away on a form you call a "problem." *Every problem* represents your belief in your separation from communication with One Mind.

> *The outer world is merely the reflection*
> *of your decision about the inner*

Projecting your problems as external to you is an attempt to protect yourself. However, what you thought protected you actually protected the deception your fear is based on; separation. The more you look out into your own shadow for your solution, the more problems you will find.

> *You will not find your solution in the world*
> *The world was made so you would not find a way out*

However, when you see the outer world as a reflection of your mind, you will see the opportunities to find your way through. Joining is the miracle that replaces your experience of polarity and opposition. You have been vigilant in your struggle to justify and maintain your projection of an outer world. Now you are being asked to do something different. You are being asked to give up your battle in exchange for peace. Use your projections as reflections for awareness rather than shadows of fear to defend against. Is this too much to ask?

Until you are able to look at the folly of your dilemma, you will continue to perceive conflicts as problems outside of you. Defensiveness continues as long as you believe there are problems to defend against. The awareness of your dilemma is a mighty companion to help you on your way. Courage is needed here because resistance is enormous.

The Solution

You are the maker of your dream. You have victimized yourself and become your own enemy. Your way out is to accept the problems you see as the problems you made. You cannot afford any exception on this point. For the one exception you permit allows blame to be a justifiable defense that limits your experience of your creative self.

Attack, pain and fear are devices you made
to protect you from waking from the nightmare
that justifies attack, pain and fear as real

Whether it is through depression or anger, your justification for attack is always found in your projection to look outside. To awaken from your dream, is to see the outer world as it truly is. It is your reflection. As your reflection, it was once believed to condemn you, now it is an opportunity to look within and heal. Rising above to join in the memory of One Mind can only be found within you.

To undo your dream, you will have to forgive how you perceive yourself. You will not be able to do that as long as you are in the habit of projecting your self condemnation onto others as betrayal and abandonment. Placing blame denies the need for forgiveness because it prevents you from taking responsibility for your projection. Blame is always the self-deception of what you think another has done to you. This defensive position obscures what you have done to yourself.[142] Therefore, *without exception* say to yourself;

My conflict with anyone is the result of self-deception

Because no one can do to you what you do to yourself first, the problem you believe to be a cause outside of you is your lie; it is not true.

You cannot forgive the lie you believe
Because every lie you believe you use to defend
. . . against forgiveness

Behind every lie is the truth that freely forgives it. Thus every problem you defend as outside of you (blame) is actually your opportunity to see your own self-deceit. To recognize self-deceit as valueless is to forgive what never occurred.

Summary

Who looks outside dreams
Who looks inside awakens

Carl Jung

Your outer world is a projection of what you do not want to see in your inner world. Maintaining this illusion (split mind) requires an enormous amount of energy and is the cause of all of your ongoing exhaustion, pain and fear. *You have no*

---

[142] *The Way Home; p155*

energy to allow for the experience of your creative self while you are busy defending your interpretations of your projections.

However, Truth as your natural inheritance, needs no defense to maintain. It will flow freely to the mind that honestly and openly releases the blocks to its awareness. Self-deception is your primary block. Because you projected an outer world to be an experience of space and time, you will need to use your reflection to show yourself that it is an illusion of a mind lost in self-deception.[143] Forgiveness is the opportunity to remember your creations when you begin to release the lies you have used against yourself.

> *Truth encounters no opposition*
> *because opposition implies weakness*
> *Therefore, only in Truth is there real strength*

---

[143]This is the proper and practical use of all the symbols you have empowered.

Communicating from Your Creative Self

You are Creation
What you give is always given to you

Introduction

The idea that you are a body, separate from other bodies, implies the need for communication. All forms of communication are special to you until you remember your identity in One Mind. One Mind can be described[144] as knowing a reality of One, the experience which requires no communication. Therefore, all forms of specialized communication are temporary in nature to either keep you in your fixed beliefs of separation, or as opportunities, a way through your fixed beliefs to remember the experience of One Mind.

The Basis of All Communication

In the dream, the body's eyes
may continue to see differences
But it is the healed mind
that does not acknowledge them

The task of the practitioner is to deny your client's denial of truth. This is not about confronting your client about what the truth is. It is about you, the practitioner, identifying as One Mind through your client. It is a view that looks past any sickness your client presents. That is how healing is accomplished. What you mistook as a problem in your client is now

---

[144]The experience of knowing is beyond description.

your opportunity to see it as not true. When you see beyond their illusion for them, you see beyond yours for you. Whatever problem your client presents, you can respond to it as the nothingness it is. Of course, you take your client where they are at with the symbols of sickness they present, but the gift your client offers is the opportunity for you to join with them towards peace of mind.

Your client must heal themselves, for the truth is in them. Yet, having obscured the truth, the light of your mind will recognize the light in their mind. This is the basis of all communication. It is a support beyond words.

Communication's Creative Purpose

What appears to come from the outside is really a reflection of your thoughts. You are caught in a loop, thinking you are listening to another when you are primarily listening to your own interpretation of people, places and things. Shared communication becomes the means to break through this loop of denial.

The creative purpose of communication is to provide information from beyond your self-defeating loop of symbolic meanings. Because truth is an experience beyond information, all forms of external communication do not convey truth. They are symbols of power to facilitate your opportunity to remember your natural state of One Mind. Therefore, in the world of the externally seeking wanderer, the primary purpose of all forms of communication is to remind you to look inward for your answer to all issues.

If the information conveyed to you or through you
does not remind you to look within for truth,
disregard it, for it is but another form of delay

Shared communication is truth's standard because truth realized is shared by all. This book is not truth. It is information channeled via paper and ink. Perhaps its message will help you remember your natural state of communication.

Types of Communication

Everything the world is
is but a symbol of your belief in separation
The miracle is
your reinterpretation of all that you allow . . . as joining
Until . . . all you see is the Creation of One

To create is to join. What you create, you will extend as a unified goal of peace. However, a split mind will project conflict. The interpretation of your world always takes the forms of what you think. Whether your expressions represent joining or separation, they are always symbolic of what you think. This is more unconscious than you realize.

Sign language, photography, art, graphs, charts, diagrams, numbers, music, smoke signals, technology, body language, the internet and even these words are just a few of an innumerable list of forms that individual minds use to attempt to bridge the space between minds separated by the illusion of substitutions.

"We were talking, about the space between us all
And the people, who hide themselves
behind a wall of illusion"

George Harrison
Within You Without You

Verbal and written communication is the most commonly used forms of bridging the space between separate minds. It seems necessary as long as you perceive yourself to be an individual mind in an individual body. From this mindset, words are used to identify, compare, define, limit, conceptualize, analyze and judge (just to name a few) in order to convey meaning. These symbols create alliances and bridge differences as much as they describe differences and create power struggles.

It is important to note that *any meaning that seems to be presented to you from a seemingly separate individual is actually the meaning you give it.* If you are not aware that you are listening to the meanings you impose on words and sounds that seem to come from the outside, you will not realize how lost you are in your own projection of a self limiting experience.[145] All communication that breaks through your projection of limited meanings is the expression from your creative self. It is a reinterpretation of your limits of thought that opens you to a glimpse of a Self larger than you. It also reminds you that;

All healing is about joining

These epiphanies, peak experiences, realizations are suspensions of beliefs that heal your peculiar idea of separation.

Telepathy is a form of communication that transfers thoughts by means other than normal sensory impressions and receptors. It is a form of communication of which every-

---

[145]Healer, that is why you never react to anyone. You merely react to your own interpretation of what another's message represents in your mind. Use whatever tools are at your disposal to teach your client that their healing comes from within themselves . . . so you can remember it yourself.

one is capable. As a matter of fact, you are constantly communicating on a level beyond thoughts and beliefs. You don't recognize this ability because you have limited your awareness of your part in the whole to an individual body-self idea. Telepathic communication is a glimpse of the Self we all share. As with any form of channeling, telepathic communication is temporary, dependent on time. Through the experience of One Mind full communication is recognized.

Because the experience of One Mind is your inheritance, your potential to remember full communication is inevitable. You meet the conditions for this experience when you selectively perceive only the forms that reflect joining. Communicating through your Creative Self involves a willingness to see only commonality and wholeness in everything you look upon. This ability overlooks all thoughts and judgments that would limit your mind to an individual experience of separation.

What is the experience of telepathic communication? The joining with another through the recognition of thoughts you already share.

An open mind is like a mirror when it sees itself in another
Here is where real communication is recognized as itself

Channeling is a specialized form of telepathic communication. There are two types of conductors for channeling.

The **trans-medium** is passive during the exchange of information. They simply pass it on. However, though the trans-medium may be given over as an open channel, that does not mean the source is a pure transmitter. The source's purpose is determined by its goal. Is the message about joining or division?

Any source that does not use symbols of power as a means to release you, is about cultivating a dependency as your guide. This is not a pure transmitter. If the message does not direct you towards peace of mind,[146] it is not a pure channel. Somewhere the ego snuck in resulting in the use of a message to perpetuate a need for a savior outside of you. A pure transmitter's intent is always for healing. Its goal is peace of mind.

The *intuitive reader* subjectively participates in the channeled information. They are aware of the messages, symbols or images they receive from their client. Seeing their client as One Mind with them, they reflect interpretations of healing; interpretations that facilitate the opportunity for their client to rise above their limiting symbol of belief.

The temptation for intuitive readers is to change or hold back information for personal or professional purposes. It is easy to present messages that are pleasing, especially when one considers that clients may be unwilling to return to the bearer of disturbing news. Intuitive readers are also prone to engage in superficial questions that side step the real issue.

For the intuitive reader, the pressure to pacify can be so strong that they may compromise the message. Without the centering strength to trust their impressions, they can become dependent on a censoring / editing process to the point where they get lost in their own spin.[147] Failing to trust Source, the intuitive reader becomes little more than what appears to be a charlatan.

If "nothing" comes to you, tell your client "nothing comes to me." Likewise, if you are centered beyond the lure of the

---

[146]The symbols that lend themselves towards a unified direction of peace of mind are the aids that help you remember your experience of truth.

[147]Adding your own spin is different than interpreting the client's symbols in a way that frees them.

ephemeral, the symbols you interpret for another will reflect opportunities for unity and forgiveness and thus healing. This principle, consistently applied, is what makes you a healed healer.

Physician, Heal Thyself

To interact openly with your client is to look beyond the sickness they present. When you look beyond their sickness to the wholeness they are, you reflect a message of healing. Why? Because, when you see your projection in another as the spark you are, you transcend the illusion of space that seems to be between you.[148] In other words, when you see yourself in the client you encounter, you move towards the memory of One Mind.[149] This is what is meant by "Physician, heal thyself."

All healing is about joining

This is the experience of the spiritual relationship. With this experience of joining, you can never fully buy into what the world seems to offer.

The Commitment

To communicate from your Creative Self is to allow the love that flows through you to be reflected by another. Let all barriers down so you may see the love you are reflected through another. Any limitation you impose on the message you send, is a message of limitation you send to yourself.

---

[148]The illusion of space is a junk yard filled with all the substitutions, limiting beliefs, symbols of power your mind has devised to deceive itself into believing in the experience of an individual reality.

[149]To commiserate with, gossip about and blame is not identifying with another as much as it is an ego alliance. This is because it does not lend itself to peace of mind.

Because you are One Mind
The gift you give to another
Is always given to you

It is only fear that limits your expression of your creative self. Release yourself as a naturally uninhibited channel, limitless in Source . . . and through all that you do, think and say . . . receive your love freely.

Summary

Teacher, your idea of a separate identity selectively perceives your experiences as different from everyone else. However, healing is the joining that transcends the illusion of individual differences. The form any event takes will be different, it always is, but the experience of healing is understood by all.

The illusion of different experiences makes it necessary for you to engage in and exchange symbolic meanings called communication. You use information from sources you perceive as outside of you to facilitate the completion of a picture for your client. Because it is always a teaching opportunity for you to learn, what you are really doing is trying to complete a picture of yourself through your client while your client is trying to complete a picture of themselves through you.

To forget you already participate in One Self is to look elsewhere for who you are not. All forms of communication exist because you believe you are a body separate from another body. Though the illusion of space between bodies seems to exist, Mind continues as One. It is for you to let go of all meanings you have placed between you and your client so those symbols can be reinterpreted to remember the truth of what you are.

You are Creation
What you give is always given to you

You need your client to remind you of this. When you remember Source, external forms of communication are no longer necessary.

Spiritual Guides

Spiritual guides symbolize any form outside of you that you believe holds answers you don't have. Somehow they seem to hold wisdoms you don't possess. You have to ask for help, interpret the directions and trust the advice. Yet if wisdom is truth, it is accessible to all. It can't be held back, hidden or partially revealed. You perceive a need for spiritual guides as long as you think you are separate from your Source of Wisdom.

In working with clients who seek spiritual guides, teach them to remember that guides are symbols of knowledge that all possess. If a guide reminds you to look within for the solution, the place where the problem was made, they are helpful. Use the symbols of power your client presents as a means to move beyond all symbols. Beyond the need for symbols is your disposition of One Mind.

I send you!
I send you on a journey
This journey is one you make in your own way
. . . at your own pace

Until you see where your path begins
You will wander aimlessly and endlessly . . .
. . . through space and time
Attracted by innumerable forms . . . symbols of magic

When you desire above all else
To awaken from your dream . . . to be Home
You will be Home
For I send you back to You!

Appendix

"For there is nothing good or bad
But thinking makes it so"

William Shakespeare
Hamlet Act 2, Scene2

Song & Dance

Reflections

Beyond the Veil

Song & Dance

When it comes to things we cherish, there are many. For example, the birth of a baby, the accomplishment of a goal, advancement in a job, a raise in pay, the recognition of a job well done, the accumulation of toys, friendship, someone to love, someone saying "I love you," and above all else, the belief in a physical body as "me." Though you might prefer one thing over another, your preference does not make the illusion more real.

> *All illusions are one*
> *One is not more real than another*

Something that I have personally cherished and strongly identified with when all the economics, politics and theologies of the world seem crazy was the honoring of Mother Earth and Mother Earth teachings.[150]

I love a story around a fire.
I love when Venus greets me in the morning or evening sky.
I love a walk through the woods.
I love the change of seasons . . . the color of fall . . .
    the falling leaves.
I love the phases of the moon.
I love to float down a wilderness stream.
I love the power of a storm.
I love how Mother Earth knows how to be.

---

[150] *The Way Home; p23*

Even still, the earth is not a place of perfection. Nor is it evolving into perfection. As a matter of fact, the earth is a place where perfection is impossible. The earth may look like it is evolving into perfection, however; it is "ashes to ashes and dust to dust."

All illusions are one
One is no more real than another

In the light of this:

Everything the world is, is but a dance

You dance in your slumber, you dance in your dreams
You dance when you whisper, you dance when you scream

You dance with a touch, you dance with your eyes
You dance when you walk, you dance when you hide

You dance to get down, you dance to get high
You dance to a dirge, you dance when you die

There isn't anything in this world you do not dance to
For this journey through is but one big song and dance
So make a nice tune to dance through
Make it a celebration of life!

Reflections

Simply stated, words reflect what you believe. Not only do the words you use symbolize the beliefs you hold dear, you also respond to the meanings you give to words that another uses. Words mean different things to different people. No wonder misunderstanding abounds.

At times, words seem to bring new information to you. Other times, the words you encounter seem to illicit a response or stir an emotional memory. Whether clearly seen or not, your response to any word is a reflection of what was already inside you. How you respond to your reflection is your expression of what you think of you. What follows here are symbols of expression known as poetry. Allow the words to remind you of what you have hidden from your view.

The Time of In-Between

The time of In-between
Is it merely just a dream?

A dream of joy, a dream of sorrow
A dream of fear waiting on tomorrow

A dream of hate, a dream of love
A dream from the stars to rise above

What is this dream of in-between?
It is your time . . . to dream

Elements

Earth: Solid and true, steady to the touch
     . . . Mother remains herself

Fire: Fire purifies, not out of pain
     But because fire burns through
     What is not you

Water: Peace is easy
     Like a cool mountain stream
     Yields through rock formations
     . . . And keeps moving

Air: Like the heart of a thunderstorm
     The calm of a hurricane's eye
     The colors of a sunset's splendor
     Air remains . . .
     Unpredictably awesome

No Man's Land

Caught in the middle, the edge of night
Something is moving, but I'm out of sight

Anticipating . . . a friend or foe
It makes little difference, when it's my time I'll know

The lots cast before me, destinations all planned
Show me your answer, please if you can

Lost in the middle, alone in the dark
Projecting life's riddle, or igniting one's spark

Courage

In between dark and light
are desires to fight

In between hot and cold
are the thoughts that make me old

In between good and bad
are days to feel sad

In between right and wrong
are opportunities to sing a song

In between up and down
my feet are on the ground

In between fight or flight
my head's drained of might

In between birth and death
I seek a moments rest

In the Arms of God

Turbulent flows the mountain stream
Deep and dark its torrents
While subtle pools of sorrow gather
From its twisting current

I set my tent at valley's edge
From where the river winds
Beneath the pools of sorrows gates
Lies the path that I must climb

I take my compass, water and food
To help me when it's time
My compass fails, my food turns stale
My water left behind

So I drink deep and long
From the torrents of my heart
Ever pushing through my fears
All I see is dark

Unexpected and unlooked for
Places of rest I find
Relief it is, temporarily
From the shadows of my mind

I cannot rest for very long
In a place I feel alone
So I push on and on
Seeking shelter from my storm

Forgetting what I was looking for
I was totally lost it seemed
I found myself in the arms of God
Awoken from my fitful dream

I Am You

I am the wind
Whispering through your mind
Through the dust of time

I am the ocean
Mysterious and deep
With secrets mine to keep

I am the mountain
Standing tall and true
With no easy way through

I am the river
Through you I start
Back to my heart

I am you

Beyond the Veil

A realization is the experience of expansive release. It is recognition beyond the limits you have given your mind to experience. The body's senses are not a part of this experience.

In having psychic experiences, do not under-estimate the power of your mind to facilitate deception. Be aware of a desire to want to repeat these experiences. They are not something extra special. It is not secret wisdom given only to a few.

I asked and was told, "It is not for you to know." With defiance, I stepped down to enter through a big wooden door representing where the Akasha records were. I was denied access. The next instant I found myself as a spark of light darting around inside a caterpillar. The caterpillar dissipated . . . and I was pure light.

1985

Beware of the idea of a place of Wisdom outside of You. The Akasha records are within you. With this in mind, freely engage in your experiences as a means to move beyond them.

Vision Quest

"I saw myself on the central mountain of the world, the highest place, and I had a vision because I was seeing in the sacred manner of the world." The sacred mountain was Harney Peak in South Dakota. And then he says, *"But the central mountain is everywhere."*

Black Elk

There is a place in the outer world that meets the inner . . . the place where movement and noise is stilled . . . the place where the ever-changing meets the eternal . . . the place where . . . "You are the central mountain, and the central mountain is everywhere."[151]

---

[151]The Power of Myth, Joseph Campbell; p89

Once Before

I saw her! It was the day before yesterday, the 20th of December.

She was simply parking her car, that's all. The setting sun touching her face . . . caught me off guard. Her beautiful auburn hair . . . such an earthly silhouette . . . was outlining her now shining facial tones . . . and the golden browns lit up her face. It overwhelmed me.

At that moment, I felt as if I was going through a whole autumn . . . an autumn I had gone through with her, as if . . . as if we met once before . . . in another life.[152]

I was afraid to entertain this thought. But it was too late. I was taken by surprise. The thoughts and feelings that overwhelmed me I could not defend against. I looked again . . .

In that moment she captured me . . . and I loved it. I openly and unabashedly gazed at her.

I took this experience into my private world. Oh, how unsettling this is.

12/22/85

---

[152]Past body recollection

All Are Called

I saw the moon rising in my mind (or was it the sun?). From right to left it rose. As it arched out of the horizon it grew into a fiery red mass . . . and then quickly settled into a well formed yellow circle.

When it reached its peak, it stopped and vibrated. Pulsating light waves radiated from its sphere like the ripples of a stone thrown into a clear calm lake.

Then it quickly shrunk back, into a white light . . . beckoning me to come.

I stepped forward . . . but I could not make the journey. I could not yet take everyone with me.

1/21/86

The Desert of Colorless Dreams

I saw within me . . . a hole . . . a black center
Around that center was a desert . . .
. . . A desert of colorless dreams . . .
There was no bush, no mountain, nothing around me . . .
. . . I saw nothingness . . .
There was nothing to touch me
And I was perfectly safe

4/6/86

The Power of the Void

I touched the power of the void . . .

The chaos of the earth surrounded me as water swelled up and pounded the rocks around me. The splash of cold water kissed my brow as if to say "I am a friend . . . but understand me, my kiss can kill those unaware . . . those who take me for granted."

I touched the power of the void . . . as the mind tamed the body's senses. Senses which are part of the body . . . a body which is part of the void.

Stand by your edge . . .

Feel the power of wind and waves crashing upon the rocks around you. Embrace this power . . . take it in . . . feel it . . . let it shake your very foundation to the bone. Let it tempt you with its overpowering despair.

Step into the void . . .

Feel the void of power as the body's senses recoil in its fearful lick of death swelling and crashing within you. Here . . . in the void of power . . . you will find the gentle repose of peaceful Being.

On the shore of Lake Superior
6/21/86

Merging with the Light
(About the cover of the book)

Surrounded by darkness, I reached up to open a door. As the door slowly cracked open, white light spread out around its edges. I stepped forward and walked in . . . for just an instant, to my surprise, and yet not . . . I met myself at the door.

As my eyes became accustomed to the bright light, I recognized everyone I would think of in this joyful atmosphere. Some had already passed. Some were currently projecting a body on earth. In this place, all had transparent bodies.

Some came up to me and said with a smile, "I see you made it the hard way . . . while you're still living with a body on earth." They would plead, "Please talk to me when you get back to earth! I want to wake up!"[153]

I responded, "I will, yes I will, I won't forget!" I heard myself thinking this in unison with whoever was pleading with me . . . so I wouldn't forget this place . . . so I would also remember to awaken.

The still small voice said, "Listen."

11/17/87

---

[153]These conversations were all experienced without spoken words.

Beyond the Horizon of Light

Hidden in the shadow of the dark side of a planet, I effortlessly sped along the surface.[154] Hugging the planet's dark surface, I moved towards the horizon of light. The horizon gradually became a dark red, changing quickly to a bright molten red.

Suddenly, the ground fell away as I shot out over the molten yellow red horizon of the planet. Looking below, I was overwhelmed by wind driven swirls of yellow white gaseous fire. The wind driven swirls moved across what seemed an expansive ocean planet of turbulent liquid gas and fire.

Immediately I realized . . . I was looking directly into the sun over Mercury's horizon. It was a calm day. I noticed no need to protect my eyes from the light, nor my face from the heat.

3/5/88

---

[154]Astral projection.

I Met Him

I stood about twenty feet away and slightly downhill . . . looking up at this huge stone altar. The altar was about ten feet square and about eight feet high. On it was the burning of an animal sacrifice. I was not able to see the sacrifice that was burning. Off of the top of this altar rolled a curling thick smoke.

"There's got to be a better way to know God than this." I thought. At that moment, around the corner to my right, walked Jesus. I recognized him immediately. Swiftly he walked by . . . between myself and the altar. A small caravan of people hustled to catch up.

In the next instant I saw myself looking out upon a crowd over Jesus' right shoulder as he sat above them on a hillside.

1990

Wake Up!

As I was sleeping on my back, I woke up to a rattling sound. I thought someone was trying to break into the house. I tried to get up but could not move. I tried to speak but could not warn my wife. No matter how hard I tried, I was paralyzed. I was scared.

Then I saw the form of a face slowly appear, looking over me as I lay on my back. The face, unknown to me, was composed of white smoke. I did not recognize it, but it was scary. I blew at it and it dissipated. Then I woke up from the dream I thought I had already awoken from. And a voice said to me "Wake up!" . . . as if I was still sleeping.[155]

1/22/07

---

[155] *The Way Home; p192*

Glossary

Collapse of Time – The result of a particular lesson learned through forgiveness. The illusion of time is shortened between you and your memory of eternity when a particular lesson need not be repeated any more. This lesson learned is an experience beyond the senses of the ephemeral called by names such as epiphanies, peak experiences, spiritual realizations, etc. Time seems to collapse when there is one less substitution (symbol / idol of belief) between you and your memory of Source. Also referred to as a speed-up.

Dreaming – Your Spirit does not know of time and space. If you believe in time and space you deny your reality in Spirit. This is called dreaming.

Ephemeral – Movement and noise as fleeting, momentary, transient, temporary, passing, brief, short-lived, etc. In other words, life as experienced through a body.

Healing – If sickness is mind's attempt to limit itself to something it is not, healing would be a changed mind about this belief, always experienced as release. This is different than relief.

Instant Karma – Instant karma is your experience of the immediate effect of your interpretation of anything; pleasant or unpleasant in any present moment.

Karma – Memories you carry as pleasure or pain, good or bad. They are interpretations held onto as personally real.

Miracle – It is the experience of mind freed of its limiting beliefs through forgiveness. This is release, not relief. Relief is the experience of rearranging the temporary or modifying your thinking to spiritualize the illusion. When you learn or undo your particular lesson by seeing it in a different way, there is a collapse of time. This is what the miracle of release is. Now you can go on to the next lesson until you run out of lessons to undo. When this is done, reincarnation is over. You stand at the end of time, at the border of eternity. Here, your miracle is needed no more.

Paranormal – Any experience that is beyond the explanation of the five senses.

Passerby – A passerby is one in the process of withdrawing all attachments from the beliefs and investments that the world seems to offer. The passerby is aware that their experience of the illusion is not home.[156]

Placebo Effect – The mistaken belief that some form outside of you was the reason for your healing. It may have been the need of the moment, but never the reason for your experience of release.

Radical Forgiveness – Forgiveness releases all false ideas about what you think reality is. Forgiveness, properly understood, recognizes that error is merely a mistaken perception needing correction at the level of your mind, not in the projection of mind's error called the world. Forgiveness recognizes that what you thought another did to you or what you

---

[156]"Be passersby" The Gospel of Thomas; #42

thought you did to another was your misinterpretation. Out of ignorance individual thoughts and bodies clash. What do you want to make it mean?

Recollection – The memory of a past body experience i.e., reincarnation. The phrase *past life* is misleading. You only have One Life, and you share that as One Mind.

Reincarnation – The mind's dream of sequential body experiences.

Waking from the Dream – The lesson of radical forgiveness being generalized without exception to everything in the ephemeral. The process of change, of becoming, is about your journey to remember Source through your ephemeral experience. Waking up to what you already are is not about evolving. It is about waking up.

Wanderer – The wanderer is one who seeks to invest in, identify with the experience of the illusion through the symbols of the ephemeral.

Also by
Mathias Karayan

Healing the Wound;
The Family's Journey through Chemical Dependency

The Way Home;
Stories from the Master

For more information contact
Karayan Publishing
www.karayanpublishing.com

These books can also be purchased at;
BUFFALO BOOKS & COFFEE
6 Division Street
Buffalo, MN 55313
763-682-3147